Horse Economics

A Personal Finance Guide for the Horse Owner

CATHERINE E. O'BRIEN, CPA

 Trafalgar Square Publishing

North Pomfret, Vermont

First published in 2005 by
Trafalgar Square Publishing
North Pomfret, Vermont 05053

Disclaimer of Liability
The author and publisher shall have neither liability nor responsibility to any person or entity with respect to any loss or damage caused or alleged to be caused directly or indirectly by the information contained in this book. While the book is as accurate as the author can make it, there may be errors, omissions, and inaccuracies.

This book is not intended as a substitute for professional advice. It is sold with the understanding that the author is not engaged in rendering financial, accounting, tax, insurance, legal or other professional advice or services. Relevant laws vary from state to state and the tax laws are constantly changing, which makes financial and tax planning difficult, therefore, please consult with a competent professional. The information in this book is based on the Internal Revenue Code and Internal Revenue Service publications available as of September 2004. The information and worksheets as well as copies of contracts and agreements provided herein are intended for educational and informational purposes only. C. E. O'Brien and Trafalgar Square Publishing are not responsible for any actions taken or damages resulting from reliance on information contained in this book, or for any inadvertent error, omission or inaccuracy contained in *Horse Economics*. Any likeness or similarity to a real event or person for examples used in this book is purely coincidental.

Disclaimer of Warranty
For this book, the author and Trafalgar Square Publishing specifically disclaim any implied warranties of merchantability or fitness for a particular purpose. No warranty may be created or extended by sales representatives or written promotional material of any kind.

Library of Congress Cataloging-in-Publication Data

O'Brien, C. E. (Catherine E.)
  Horse economics : a personal finance guide for the horse owner / C.E. O'Brien.
    p. cm.
  ISBN-13: 978-1-57076-319-9 (pbk.)
  ISBN-10: 1-57076-319-4 (pbk.)
  1. Finance, Personal. 2. Horses. 3. New business enterprises. 4. Horse industry. I. Title.
  HG179.O23 2005
  332.024'0088'798—dc22
                                         2005008507

Grateful acknowledgement to the Virginia State Corporation Commission for the use of information and terms contained in their consumer guides.

Book and cover design by Heather Mansfield
Typeface: AGaramond and Perpetua

Front cover image of DHR Quite a Time (Comet); back cover of the author and Comet; photography by Rita Root

Printed in the United States of America

10 9 8 7 6 5 4 3 2 1

DEDICATION

To Brio, a genuine friend and companion for most of my life.
He provided stability and peace in a sometimes chaotic world.
His noble heart will not be forgotten.

TABLE OF CONTENTS

ACKNOWLEDGMENTS

First and foremost, I thank my husband, who, when asked if he wanted a copy of the book replied, "Why do I need one? I have already read each chapter twenty times with pen in hand!" Thanks to Mom and Dad and special thanks to all who supported my ideas, gave willingly of their time and endured my questions in order to bring this book together. Among them were: Jeffrey Zwerdling, Esquire and Brett Zwerdling, Esquire, with the Law Offices of Zwerdling & Oppleman, P.C., Robert Harper with the Virginia Cooperative Extension Service, Greg B. Farmer, President and Chief Executive Officer of Colonial Farm Credit, ACA, Thomas Newton, DVM, Denise Gorondy, DVM, Ernest M. Swartz, MSW, Junior Johnson, Bet Poarch, Joel Groover, Albert Myers, Thom Trout, Nicole McCabe, Esquire, and Mike Roane, CPA, Jeff Love, CPA, Greg Forman, CPA and Elizabeth Amos, CPA with Mitchell, Wiggins & Company, LLP, Certified Public Accountants and Consultants. Lastly, I appreciate the staff at Trafalgar Square. Caroline Robbin's additions and organizational contributions were most helpful, and Rebecca Schmidt's patience, hard work, and sense of humor made the process enjoyable.

CHAPTER ONE

Open Your Heart... and Your Wallet

THE PERSONAL MEANING OF HORSE OWNERSHIP

Deciding to purchase a horse ranks up there with getting married or buying a house—it can be just as expensive as either of those undertakings. I have had horses since I was fourteen, and as a financial analyst, I now realize that if I had saved and invested all the money I have spent on horses over the years, I could be rich! However, the wealth of satisfaction and enjoyment gained from having horses in my life far outweighs the *time value of money*✦.

Due to the time and financial commitment it demands, horse ownership is not a hobby, it is a lifestyle; it doesn't matter whether you own your own farm or board your horse at a stable. A horse acts as an "identifier" or image enhancer: as a horse owner, you consider yourself a horseman or horsewoman. The horse activities you engage in and the clothes you wear—from the ropers, jeans, and cowboy hat to the field boots, riding helmet, and hunt coat—help you to define the view you have of yourself. The mud on your shoes, the horsehair on your coat, and the green slime on your sleeve complement your style.

Horses and the activities associated with them have a very significant social aspect for the people involved, as well. Shows, clinics, riding clubs, and rodeos, to name a few, allow you to share a common interest with others and can make you feel as if you are accepted by, and belong to a group of people. Children can reap great benefits from being involved

> **SO YOU KNOW...**
>
> ✦ The *time value of money* is one of the fundamental concepts in financial management. The saying, "A dollar today is worth more than a dollar tomorrow" is true because you can invest and earn interest on your dollar today. The earlier you start, the more your funds will grow.

with a 4-H club, taking instruction, joining a riding team, and developing friends at their riding stable. They can learn teamwork, cooperation, and responsibility, not to mention how to care for and manage their horse. Such skills translate well into other areas of their lives.

Though all pets can have similar positive effects on their owners, it is important to understand that having a horse is *not* like having a dog. A dog will forgive you regardless of the treatment he receives. For example, you can unintentionally hurt your dog's feelings when you leave for work each day. I have a terrier that pouts on weekday mornings, but every evening when I return, I get this tail-wagging, toy-bone-holding, exuberant "she's home" dance. Obviously, the dog forgot that he was upset that morning.

However, in my experience, this is not the case with horses. I distinctly remember one night when I reached for the horse "cookie jar" in the barn, only to realize (to my horror) that I had not filled it and did not have any back-up treats. Since all eyes had seen me pick up the jar, I was in trouble. The next morning at feeding time, I was met with indifference from some and even downright disgust from one horse (the same horse that throws a fit when I pay attention to another and when he thinks he is going to be left out of an activity). This illustrates how horses have the capability of holding grudges. Emotional and physical experiences affect them for longer periods of time because of their capacity for memory, emotion, and self-preservation. Horses don't automatically trust you, and every horse has his own distinct personality and quirks.

A horse's ability to interact and bond with humans comes from accepting a person, not just as a part of the herd, but the leader of it. You have to *earn* a horse's respect; it cannot be achieved through coercion or trickery. Once you gain your horse's trust through consistency and fairness, your relationship can develop. When you have a horse that is excited to see you walk in the barn and enjoys being ridden, then you know you have succeeded in being a good horseman, which can bring immense satisfaction and feelings of accomplishment.

Of course, the trade-off for these good feelings is the amount of money you spend attaining them. You not only need to know how to make the horse-ownership lifestyle enjoyable, but feasible, as well. Whether you are a devoted parent fulfilling a horse-crazy child's dream, or an adult purchasing your very first horse, this chapter is designed to give you some insight as to how much horse you can afford. Quite often, people only consider the purchase price of the horse and maybe the cost of boarding at a local stable. I feel a better approach is to have some idea of all the costs involved with maintaining a horse in order to then determine how much can be budgeted toward the purchase price.

The recurring costs associated with horse ownership can be managed within your budget as long as you are aware of what they are, and plan and account for them. In the following pages, you'll find I've listed seven areas of horse-related expenditure to give you some idea of where your money will go. In addition, I walk you through the process of actually purchasing a horse. My hope is that by arming you with this information at the outset, you will be better prepared to tackle specific monetary issues I discuss later in this book.

SEVEN AREAS OF EXPENDITURE

1. Stabling Arrangements

For those who own, or plan to own a farm, I discuss the potential costs of keeping your horse at home in great detail in chapter 3, and developing a horse property in chapter 5. If not, chances are you will be boarding out your newest family member. You will need to compare potential boarding stables before purchasing a horse. Find local stables by talking with riding instructors, veterinarians, and managers of local tack shops. Regional horse magazines and newsletters often have listings of stables in your area. As of the time of writing, boarding fees range from $200 to $900 a month, depending on your location (some parts of the United States are much more expensive than others in all the topics I discuss in this book) and what the facility includes in that price. Keep in mind that some services incur extra charges. To learn more about choosing a boarding stable, see page 62.

2. Necessary Routine Care

There are three main areas of routine horse care that you will have to take into account, whether your horse is stabled at home or boarded out.

Hoof Care

A blacksmith or farrier must trim, or trim and shoe your horse's hooves every five to eight weeks. (During periods of rain and good pasture growth, five to six weeks is normal in some areas of the United States; in the winter months when hoof growth slows, every six to eight weeks can be adequate, depending on the horse.) Each foot needs to be trimmed properly, removing excess toe and balancing the hoof. Shoes need to provide ample support and be left wide enough to accommodate hoof growth and expansion until the next appointment with the farrier.

The cost of a trim ranges from $20 to $30, trim and two front shoes from $50 to $75, and trim and four shoes from $75 to $150 (larger horses may cost more). If your horse needs extra hoof care and special shoes or procedures performed, expect to pay more.

This is the one area of care I never skimp. The old saying, "No hoof, no horse," is one that is very true.

Veterinary Care

Typically, a riding horse will require two visits a year from a veterinarian for routine medical care, which includes vaccinations for rabies, tetanus, Potomac Horse Fever, West Nile Virus, rhinopneumonitis, equine influenza, strangles (Streptococcus), and Eastern and Western encephalomyelitis. Depending on where you live, your veterinarian may recommend additional vaccinations, such as Venezuelan encephalomyelitis. Some of these shots are given once a year, and others are repeated in six months to ensure immunity. The veterinarian may also draw blood to perform a Coggins test for *Equine Infectious Anemia*✦.

A horse's teeth should be checked once a year. Floating, which is the filing and shaping of the teeth by a veterinarian or qualified equine dental practitioner, takes off sharp points that may occur from aging and the horse's grinding and chewing food. Sharp points can make the horse uncomfortable, interfere with the function of the bit, and hinder proper digestion.

> **SO YOU KNOW...**
>
> ✦ *Equine Infectious Anemia*—also known as "swamp fever"—is a highly contagious and potentially fatal, blood-borne viral disease.

Combined, the annual visit and follow-up for vaccination boosters, tooth floating, and Coggins test can cost between $200 and $400. Most equine veterinarians are mobile and come to your farm or stable. The travel charge or trip fee ranges from $15 to $50, becoming higher the farther they travel.

Worming

Horses need to be wormed (or "dewormed") at least every eight weeks. Alternating types of wormers (different "classes") helps to prevent parasites from developing resistance to the medications. There are numerous brands of paste wormer on the market; however, it is important to compare the ingredients and note which parasites will be affected. A paste wormer costs between $6 and $13 in most tack and feed stores or livestock supply catalogs.

3. Feeding and Supplementation

Commercial pelleted grains and sweet feed usually cost between $7 and $15 per 50-pound bag. Hay ranges from $3 to $9 per 55-pound bale, and one horse can consume 100 or more bales a year, depending on climate and the quality of your pasture. When you board out all feed and hay is usually included in your board fee. Supplements are an additional cost and depend on the individual horse. Typically, a pleasure horse that gets a quality commercial grain mixture, plenty of hay, and a mineral salt block will not need extra vitamins and minerals, though he may need one or more hoof or joint supplements. (Your veterinarian will help you determine your horse's extra needs.) For example, I have an older horse that needs joint supplementation; a six-month supply of Cosequin® costs $150 to $220 depending on where purchased.

4. Supplies, Tack, and Accessories

Having a horse means lots of "stuff"! The very basic beginner's kit may include, but is not limited to, the following:

> Rubber curry comb
> Hoof pick with brush
> Hard brush, medium brush, and soft brush
> Regular human hair brush (for manes and tails)
> Large-toothed comb
> Sweat scraper and shedding blade
> Cheap towels
> Plastic tote
> Hoof conditioner
> Shampoo, conditioner, and hair polish
> Fly spray

Liniment

Wound dressing

Wonder Dust®

Epsom® salt

Gauze and wrap

Clippers

Halter and cotton leads

Turnout blanket

Splint boots and bell boots

Shipping boots

This kit will cost $300 to $400, depending on brands and vendors chosen. Equine supply catalogs are good places to start (see *Resources*, p. 218).

Saddles and other pieces of tack are riding discipline-specific and require "shopping around" for the best prices. The saddle has to fit both the horse and the rider, so enlist the help of your instructor, your veterinarian, and your local tack shop owner to find a saddle that suits for a reasonable price. For example, an average good quality hunt seat saddle will cost $600 to $1200. Add stirrups and stirrup leathers, an English bridle, snaffle bit, girth, and saddle pad to complete your basic turnout for another $200 to $400, depending on brands. A Western trail or pleasure saddle will cost $300 to $450 for synthetic and $800 to $1500 for traditional leather (silver-detailed, roping, and barrel racing saddles are more expensive.) Add a bridle, tom-thumb or regular snaffle, breastplate, girth, and saddle pad to complete your ensemble for another $250 to $500.

5. Riding Instruction

For a child and a novice, adult horse owner, I recommend regular riding instruction. Bet Poarch, a *trainer*⁺ and *instructor*⁺ who specializes in hunters and jumpers with over 40 years of teaching experience, says she often receives a phone call from a man who wants to buy a horse for his wife, or a parent a pony for a child. Frequently, they ask about riding lessons beforehand. Ms. Poarch tells them, "I would not buy a horse without taking riding lessons first, anymore than I would go to the airport and rent a plane without taking flying lessons first!" Horses can be dangerous animals and inexperience is almost a sure way to get hurt.

An instructor can help you become a better rider and horse person, and can also assist in the purchase of a new horse. Further, an instructor can give you some idea of the costs involved in tack and apparel designed specifically for the discipline you are interested in pursuing, as well as what it will cost to compete at horse shows in your area.

Lesson prices vary by instructor, and most have different fees for private lessons and group lessons. These range from $25 to $75 per hour for a private and $15 to $60 for a group lesson. Finding the best, affordable instructor available will take some effort and you may have to try several before you find one that fits your personality, skill level, and budget.

6. Insurance

While most horse owners who ride for pleasure or low-level competition do not need specialty equine insurance, there are several types of insurance coverage available for particular situations. For example, when the purchase price of a horse is sizeable and the money to replace him hard to come by, equine mortality and medical/surgical coverage can be obtained (see p. 45).

Premiums for these policies vary according to breed, age, and use of horse, and are not usually cost-prohibitive. The mortality/theft coverage premium for most pleasure horses is approximately 3 to 3.5 percent of the purchase price, and the estimated average for medical/surgical coverage (less than $10,000 annual limit) is around $250. So, a four-year-old, registered Thoroughbred mare purchased for $15,000 and used for novice-level eventing would cost $775 per year to fully insure ($15,000 x 3.5 percent = $525. Adding on a medical/surgical premium of $250 = $775).

Another thing to consider is that most property and casualty insurer's homeowner policies do not cover equine-related exposures (i.e., liability and defense costs for property damage and bodily injury caused by your animal). Therefore, it is prudent to purchase a personal horse owner's liability policy. These can cost from $225 to $500 per year (most will cover one to three horses without additional premium), with an aggregate coverage limit ranging from $1.5 to $3 million. (See chapter 2 for an in-depth discussion of your different insurance options.)

SO YOU KNOW…

✦ For clarification, the term *instructor* refers to someone who teaches riding lessons and focuses on the rider's skills.

✦ A *trainer* is someone who primarily works with the horse or both horse and rider. Often, where one term is used in this book, the other may be substituted.

7. Emergencies

"Just because you can afford the maintenance on a horse, doesn't mean that you can afford one," says Denise A. Gorondy, DVM. Dr. Gorondy has a veterinary practice with Virginia Equine Clinic in Manakin, Virginia. "What happens to new horse owners is an extensive injury involving $2,000 to $3,000 and this is a wake-up call for them."

An injury can happen to any horse. A common example: a horse steps on a nail and punctures the *navicular bursa*✦. This requires surgery, long-term antibiotics, sterile bandaging, and special shoeing while the horse recovers. Or, a horse walks into a branch under the tree in his pasture and suffers a puncture wound to the eye—with a secondary fungal infection. According to Dr. Gorondy, the oral anti-fungal medications cost over $100 per day and are prescribed for a long period of time.

Clearly, you need to set up an emergency fund in the event of your horse suffering a serious injury or getting *colic*✦. The purchase of medical/surgical coverage can relieve some of the financial worry (see p. 45), but "older" horses (normally described as over the age of fifteen) are not insurable, and many beginning riders start out with older—wiser—horses. Regardless of your horse's age, I recommend putting aside $150 per month in a savings account, or keeping a credit card with a zero balance, to use in the event of a horse emergency.

> **SO YOU KNOW...**
>
> ✦ The *navicular bursa* is a fluid-filled sac that acts as a cushion between the deep flexor tendon and the navicular bone in the horse's hoof.
>
> ✦ *Colic* is abdominal pain or digestive disorder in the horse; it has many causes and is considered very serious.

PURCHASING A HORSE

When you are purchasing your first horse, you need someone with experience to guide you and be the voice of reason. Enlist an instructor or trainer you trust to evaluate a horse before—and after—purchase. While you may be lucky enough to have a knowledgeable friend who will help you horse-hunt for free, most instructors expect to be compensated for their time and travel. You can expect to pay from $15 to $50 an hour for their efforts.

Define Your Riding Goals

In addition to finding a good trainer to help you evaluate a prospective horse, it is important to clarify your personal riding goals. Thom Trout, head trainer and director of the Riding Academy at the Essex Equestrian Center in West Orange, New Jersey (the largest equestrian center on the East Coast), oversees twelve instructors and more than 100 horses. He specializes in finding the right horse for junior, amateur, and professional riders. Mr. Trout says, when looking for a horse to buy "…many people have a marvelous grasp of the insignificant. They focus on one or two things that are really unimportant in the scheme of things instead of looking at their overall goals and objectives in their riding."

Do you intend to compete at a certain level? Do you want an experienced horse that has already proven himself in the ring? Do you want a mount that challenges you? Or, do you want a super quiet horse that will accept your current level of riding skill? These are important questions to answer before starting your search.

Evaluating a Prospect

Another key element to making a sound purchase decision is asking the seller questions to see if a prospective horse will indeed be right for you. A horse can be a perfect physical specimen, but his personality could be incompatible with your own and render him less than a joy to work with and ride. Questions should include:

- How long have you owned the horse?

- What is your reason for selling?

- What is the horse's training and ability? What is the horse currently used for?

- Does the horse bite, kick, crib, or weave? Does he chew wood?

- How does the horse behave while riding in a group of horses or in the show ring?

- When were the horse's last shots, worming, and farrier visit?

- How does the horse behave for the farrier and vet?

- Is the horse sound for all uses?

- What is the horse's history of injury or illness?

- Has the horse ever foundered, colicked, or had his hocks or other joints injected?

- Any eye or vision problems currently, or in the past?

- Any respiratory problems?

- Does the horse require any special hoof care, corrective trimming or shoeing?

- What and how much grain is the horse fed? What type of hay? Any supplements?

- Is he an easy loader? What type of trailer? How does he travel?

- What is his behavior around dogs, children, and farm equipment?

Study the horse as he is handled by the seller, and see how he goes under saddle before you attempt to ride him yourself. While watching him perform, ascertain:

- How are the horse's ground manners?

- Does the horse appear to tolerate grooming and bathing?

- How does he act in the pasture and stable around other horses?

- How does he react to tacking up and tightening the girth?

- What type of saddle is used? Does he need any special pads?

- What type of leg protection?

- Does the horse stand still when being mounted?

- Behave with other horses and riders coming and going?

- Does the rider need to use a lot of leg?

- Is the horse touchy and sensitive, or forgiving to the rider's aids?

- Does the horse stop from all gaits when asked?

- When riding in an open field or on the trail, does he respond and stop?

- Is he suitable for a beginner?

The answers to these questions can provide some insight into the temperament and behavior of the horse no matter the skill level of the buyer. They also provide clues about care and maintenance issues that could increase the cost of ownership for that particular horse. Discuss all these matters and observations with your instructor and veterinarian.

Pre-Purchase Examination

I advise anyone considering the purchase of a horse to have him thoroughly examined by a veterinarian. Satisfactory results should be a condition of the sales agreement (see p. 169). In addition to providing you with valuable information about the prospective horse's condition and behavior, it also allows you to back out of the sale if there are any doubts raised. Of course, the veterinarian does not have a crystal ball and cannot guarantee the horse won't be lame a month later, but he can assess the horse's condition that day, give you his initial findings, and make recommendations for further diagnostics such as radiographs (X rays) or blood tests. The veterinarian can also screen the horse to detect any pain medication used by a seller to mask unsoundness, or tranquilizer to make the horse quiet.

Thomas J. Newton, DVM, and his wife own Little Hawk Farm in Crozier, Virginia, where they specialize in equine reproductive services. Dr. Newton recommends a pre-purchase exam—even on a "free" horse. "A person needs to know the condition of an animal before he or she takes possession to help take care of the horse properly," says Dr. Newton. He emphasizes that the focus of a pre-purchase exam is no longer on soundness alone, but on serviceability, too. It is important to have a veterinarian familiar with the type of horse you are buying, whether it is a reining horse, jumper, or broodmare. Dr. Newton also agrees that a reputable trainer should go with you to look at a prospect. "It is the trainer's responsibility to assess the suitability of the horse; it is the veterinarian's job to make sure the horse is physically serviceable," he says. "By getting both a professional trainer and a licensed veterinarian to look at the horse, the purchaser has two professionals to fall back on."

In the case of a performance horse, it is important that he perform his intended job during the exam—and the veterinarian needs to know why you are planning to purchase a horse: if you intend to get a higher value from resale, then Dr. Newton recommends radiographs be taken during this initial exam. You will then have a comparative set when another exam is performed before a resale.

The expense of the pre-purchase examination is borne by the purchaser. When asking local veterinarians their prices for necessary routine care (see p. 3), also ask about pre-purchase examinations. Prices range from $200 to $1,500, depending on how extensively the horse is examined.

Rational Purchase Decisions

Pre-purchase exams can help you make a rational decision when buying a horse. A *rational decision* is one that is thought out and alternatives are considered. Many adults fall in love with the idea of having a horse and buy the first one that comes along. This is an emotional rather than a calculated, well-thought-out decision. Dr. Newton mentions that he often sees children whose hearts are "broken" when a horse or pony doesn't pass the vet check, and parents unfortunately going along with a child's pleas rather than listening to reason.

In order to make a rational decision, it is important to consider all options. As the purchaser, you are in control, and *waiting* is an option. Instead of being in such a hurry to "own a horse" that you "settle" for a horse, or overlook serious defects, wait until you find one that you really like and that meets your other criteria. Consult experienced horse people for advice, and ask questions of the seller before you buy.

Beware the Hard Sell

Some people who buy and sell horses "target" the novice horse person. These unscrupulous dealers prey on beginners who are more likely to "fall in love" with a horse, whether due to a pretty face or because he appears to be really quiet and good with children. Frequently, they offer a horse they have only had in their barn a few days so don't know well. However, they will "assure" you the horse is bombproof! Such dealers usually sell their horses at low prices so they can move them quickly. They are wonderful salesmen—they could put a hood ornament on a Buick and sell it as a Jaguar!

I remember when I was looking for a schoolhorse suitable for teaching beginners to ride, and I was working on a shoestring budget. I wanted something quiet that would forgive riders' mistakes as they learned. I didn't need anything beautiful, just a good solid horse.

In a matter of a few weeks, I ran across several predatory marketers of horses. Their advertisements on the internet looked great, the telephone conversations were pleasant, and they seemed knowledgeable and genuine. Road trips found their facilities ranged from immaculate to horrid—though I found that the nicer the facilities, the more I was thrown off guard because I assumed that negotiations would be fair and honest.

For instance, one place I visited actually had a horse that fit the bill.

THE HARD-SELL SALES PITCH

When horse shopping, the following claims should raise a red flag:

- "At this price, the horse won't last long."
- "You had better make a decision—I have people lined up to see this horse every day this week."
- "Most of the people I sell to are just starting out, so I try to have really quiet horses."
- "My veterinarian has already looked at the horse, and he says the horse is fine."
- "I have recent pre-purchase exam records right here, so you won't need one, which will save you money."
- "The first or second person who sees this horse will buy him."

And, if you hear any of the following during negotiations, hang on to your deposit and look elsewhere:

- "I don't make sales subject to vet checks or pre-purchase exams anymore," followed by some story about how the seller lost two weeks of valuable sale time when a customer didn't end up purchasing a really great horse.
- "I'll take your deposit, but it won't hold the horse while you make arrangements for your vet. If someone sees the horse and writes me a check for the purchase amount, the horse is sold." (Then essentially, your deposit is meaningless.)
- "You can have a right of first refusal. If someone wants to buy him, I'll call you and give you the option of purchasing the horse first." (You don't know if another buyer even exists.)

The horse seemed to have a great mind and a kind eye, and I was instantly hooked. I told the seller that I wanted a veterinarian to look at him, but I was willing to put a deposit down. (Horses, like houses, do move quickly if they are desirable. Experience had taught me that if I did find a horse I liked, I should put a deposit down in an amount I could stand to lose.) At this point, several red-flag phrases were thrown at me (see sidebar). I was dumbfounded because I had not expected it. Because I really liked the horse, I pleaded with the seller to hold the horse until my vet could see him—a very reasonable request. No dice. The seller wasn't budging.

The horse was not the best mover and a little short-strided in front, which I assumed was due to his fairly upright pasterns. I held the gelding's right front leg bent for one minute, and then we trotted him off. He was lame. I flexed the other front leg and the gelding was off on that side as well. He certainly did not appear sound enough to stand up to any kind of work for any length of time.

I realized then how easily someone could get pressured into buying a horse. Because I really liked the gelding, I was a prime candidate for the "hard sell." A horse might be offered at a great price, but you need to know what soundness and maintenance issues may be awaiting. Your "cheap" horse won't be cheap if he is chronically lame requiring frequent visits from the veterinarian, pain medication, and expensive supplements every month. A reputable horse person will allow you to have a horse vetted, honor your deposit, and hold the horse for you for a reasonable amount of time.

The True Cost of an Unsuitable Horse

Unfortunately, when a new horse is purchased, he doesn't come with a guarantee that he will be a perfect match in temperament and ability for the rider. Just as people are affected and shaped by their experiences in life, a horse comes with baggage, too. Evaluating a new horse takes time, much longer than the two-week trial period prospective purchasers may be able to negotiate. Sometimes, it may take months for a horse to adjust and bond with his new owner, learn the new rider's communication style, and unlearn bad habits he may have picked up in former homes.

However, if a horse and rider are not making progress after six months, or the horse is exhibiting unexpected and dangerous behavior not caused by the handler or rider, it may be time to assess the long-term viability of the partnership. Consult your instructor and veterinarian if you are having difficulty with your new mount. You may have purchased an animal you simply don't get along with or that wasn't properly represented to you. If this is indeed the case, you should find a trainer or rider who is more compatible with your horse to work with him and prevent any bad behavior from becoming habit. The trainer can evaluate the horse, correct unwanted behaviors, and reeducate the horse, if needed. This process can either better your own relationship with the horse or facilitate the sale of the animal to a buyer who is a more appropriate match.

Clinging to a horse that is not going to work for you may cost more than just board and maintenance. While there are inherent risks in handling any horse, those risks are increased with a horse that you are afraid of, or one that exhibits particularly dangerous behavior. Plus, horse ownership is supposed to be fun. If you are not enjoying your horse and the time you spend at the barn, you are defeating the reason you purchased a horse in the first place.

YOUR DECISIONS AFFECT YOUR HORSE'S AFFORDABILITY
Cost-Benefit Analysis

"If you understand the motivation for your decisions, you can make good decisions," says Ernest M. Swartz, M.S.W., a licensed clinical social worker. According to Mr. Swartz, "balanced" persons "are self-aware and know why they are doing what they are doing." If you take this rule for your personal decisions a step further and always do a *cost-benefit analysis*—a comparison of the positive and negative aspects of a course of action— you can make good financial decisions as well.

A cost-benefit approach should be used in all resource allocation decisions. *Resources*◆, including both time and money, should only be spent if the expected benefits from using those resources will exceed the expected costs of those resources. *Benefits should outweigh costs.* In other words, if you spend a dollar, what you're spending it on should be worth more than a dollar to you.

Let's say you are flipping through the livestock catalog because you need to purchase fly spray. Do you purchase the economy brand for $4.20 per bottle, or do you purchase the premium fly spray, which lasts ten minutes longer than the economy brand, for $13.50 per bottle? If you don't ride your horse for very long, or flies don't really bother him, there is no real benefit gained from spending the extra $9.30 a bottle. However, if you have a horse that goes into a bucking fit when a fly lands on him, then the benefit justifies the extra cost (and you get to dismount in one piece.)

To give another example, perhaps you have to choose the type of fencing for a piece of land you intend to use as a paddock. Fencing an acre with three-board sections would cost approximately $1,300 (not including labor), and electric-tape fencing with wooden posts, approximately $950. Both are safe and effective for horses. If you absolutely love the idea of a wooden fence and know you will smile every time you see it

> **SO YOU KNOW...**
>
> ◆ A *resource* is a source of supply of revenue or information or something else that adds "value" to human life.

from your kitchen window, then the extra $350 is worth it. However, if you don't have an aesthetic preference, the electric tape is the better choice.

A good financial decision is one that survives cost-benefit analysis *and* fits into your *budget*. You need to have both for your choice to make sense financially. Whether you have the option to spend the $13.50 on fly spray depends on the amount of resources you have available to devote to your equine pursuits.

Does Your Decision Make Sense?

If a person making approximately $40,000 annually, boards her horse at a stable for $400 per month, takes weekly lessons, and competes twice a month at horse shows, she could easily spend over $1,000 per month. That means *40 percent* of her take-home pay is consumed by the cost of caring for her horse and related activities. That is a huge financial commitment.

Budgeting is the prioritization of your spending, which means dealing with limited resources and allocating those resources to achieve maximum utilization. Maximum utilization can only be achieved when you consider your complete financial picture. Viewing the full scope of financial goals and obligations enables you to make informed budgetary and management decisions that will benefit both you and your horse. (To learn how to create a household budget, see p. 24.)

When making an equine-related financial decision (EFD), it is helpful to ask yourself three simple questions:

1. *Does my decision benefit me?*
2. *Does my decision benefit the horse?*
3. *Does my decision make good sense financially?*

If the answer is "yes" to all three questions, chances are you're making a *good decision* for all parties involved. And, as long as the answers to numbers 1 *or* 2, as well as number 3 are "yes," then you are at least making a *financially sound decision*.

To illustrate this point, consider Dr. Denise Gorondy's example of an extremely old and debilitated horse that was in a tremendous amount of pain and could barely walk, yet the owners couldn't bear to lose him and would not end his suffering. If the couple asked themselves the three

EFD questions, they may have come to a different conclusion:

- *Did the decision to prolong the horse's life benefit the owners?* Yes. The owners were not emotionally ready to let go of the horse.

- *Did this decision benefit the horse?* No. The horse was suffering from extreme pain and could not eat properly.

- *Did this decision make sense financially?* No. It did not fit in the couple's budget, and they had to resort to paying vet bills with credit cards. And, because the horse was not a vibrant young animal with a chance of full recovery, but old and debilitated, the expected benefits of their decision did not exceed the expected costs.

Because the only "yes" was to Question 1, the owners' decision to prolong the horse's life was neither good for all parties, nor financially sound.

In a different example, Dr. Gorondy had clients whose horse suffered a puncture wound in a joint. Though they had financial resources available, the owners chose to treat the injury themselves for two weeks. By the time Dr. Gorondy was called to examine the horse, the infection had spread to the bone and there were now only two options: perform surgery, or put the horse down. Had the owners asked themselves the three EFD questions when the horse was first injured, they may not have waited as long to call the veterinarian:

- *Did the decision to treat the puncture wound involving a joint themselves benefit the owners?* Yes. They didn't like the horse and intended to sell him and buy another. They, therefore, couldn't justify spending money on a veterinarian if they didn't need to do so.

- *Did this decision benefit the horse?* No. There are some wounds an owner can safely treat, but a puncture wound involving a joint capsule is not one of them. (Puncture wounds are difficult to treat because the outer layer of skin heals over a pocket of infection that can quickly spread.)

- *Did this decision make sense financially?* No. Putting off necessary veterinary care for an injury to a critical area does not follow the principles of *asset management*. For example, the property manager of a large office building pays to have the walls painted, carpets cleaned, and landscaping maintained. These are costs associated with operating the office building and continuing the flow of rental income associated with that building. In the same way, you should manage and maintain a horse to increase his value, performance, and happiness, which will, in turn, increase the benefits you derive. Your horse is an asset to you, whether a monetary asset because of resale worth or an emotional asset due to your enjoyment of horse-related activities.

Because the only "yes" was to Question 1, the owners' decision to treat the puncture wound themselves was neither good for all parties, nor financially sound.

Brio's Story

Nothing is black and white when it comes to horses. Decisions made where the health and welfare of any animal are concerned are a complex mix of finance, ethics, and emotions, as I have experienced first-hand.

It was a late January evening around 11:30 P.M. or so, and I was washing my face and getting ready to retire when I heard a loud bang outside the house. I didn't immediately hear it again, so thinking it was the neighbor slamming a trash can lid, I crawled into bed. I had started to settle in when I heard the noise again, three times in a row, and I knew then it was coming from the barn. I shook my husband awake and said, "We have to get to the barn, something is wrong!" We bundled up and went outside where the temperature was around 15 degrees and the wind cut right through us. It was absolutely frigid.

When we got to the barn, my old gelding, Brio, had been rolling and thrashing, his blanket covered in shavings. He had been as demanding as ever at dinnertime, eaten his grain as usual, and had starting chomping his hay when I said goodnight, but now it appeared he was colicking. I ran back to the house and called my vet, explaining how bad it was and that she needed to come out to the farm. She arrived about an hour later.

The vet tubed him—a procedure where a nasal-gastric tube filled with mineral oil is inserted through his nostril and into his stomach—gave him a sedative and painkiller, and left more sedative with me to give in several hours if he did not feel better. Even though Brio was in extreme pain, he didn't offer any resistance, which was unusual for him. He had been abused and mistreated before I purchased him and really didn't think much of humankind. (In fact, he only considered a few people worthy of tolerating, and fortunately, I was lucky enough to be one of them.)

After the vet left, my husband and I returned to the house to get warm, checking Brio every 30 minutes until I heard him kicking and thrashing again. We hand-walked him and gave him more sedative and when he was quiet, we again left him so we could warm ourselves.

We hadn't even reached the house when Brio started thrashing again, so I made another call to the vet. When she arrived, she gave him more painkiller and sedative, and we made arrangements to take him to the equine hospital a little over an hour away.

At the clinic, the ultrasound revealed fatty tumors had formed and strangled a portion of Brio's small intestine. The vet explained this was common with older horses and there were often no warning signs—like a time bomb, only you don't know the clock is running. Surgery was the only option; however, with the tumors, it would be complicated, and there was no guarantee my horse would be alive when all was said and done. The vet estimated the cost to be $8,000 to $10,000, a total that would run even higher when I factored in the $1,500 I had already spent on the house calls and the follow-up care that would be necessary.

I wasn't prepared for this at all. Brio was twenty-six years old, but had been sound and healthy, and he had more fight and spunk than the seven-year-old in the barn. He didn't look his age and was still heavily muscled. I had even taught my husband to ride him over the last year or so, which they both enjoyed. I had envisioned Brio living another ten years and always thought that I would know the right time to have him put down and bury him on the farm. After all, we had been together twenty-two years, and he had always been there for me, through good times and bad.

But, there were other factors at play. Nine months before this awful day, the company where my husband worked had changed ownership, and two weeks later, his whole department was laid off. No warning. No severance package. The unexpectedness of the change in our joint income had to impact my decision-making. When you're financially stretched like a rubber band that's about to break, there is no room for error.

Brio's age, the chance of complications, and the pain he would have to endure, combined with the financial position my husband and I were in, lead me to the decision not to go through with the surgery. In the end, I couldn't even bring him home to bury him because a huge snowstorm was hitting the area, and there was no way for a contractor to get equipment to the farm. I was crushed. The blanket of white snow made the farm seem even more empty without him.

- *Did my decision not to have surgery performed benefit me?* No. I miss my horse terribly.

- *Did my decision benefit my horse?* Yes. He was in excruciating pain and the risks of complicated, possibly futile surgery were too great.

- *Did my decision make financial sense?* Yes. Choosing to incur a liability (the surgical and follow-up medical costs) with no way of paying for it would not have been a good financial decision, especially when I was responsible for the care and well-being of family and other animals.

Looking back, I know I made the right decision, but it was not an easy one. When something becomes an integral part of your everyday life and brings you great joy, it is hard to make objective decisions where that "something" is concerned. Emotions, attachment, and pride in caring for an animal all factor in to the decisions we make as horse owners. However, as in my own experience with Brio, financial considerations need to be taken into account, as well.

Financial and Risk Management

Part I
PERSONAL AND HOUSEHOLD GENERAL FINANCE

It is probably safe to say you plan and prepare in order to meet your equestrian goals—such as bringing a young horse along or competing at a higher level. It is important that you give the same attention to your personal financial goals. Begin by viewing yourself and your household as a single entity, and then decide what the "goals" for that entity should be—for instance, a corporation's goals often include maximizing profit and building shareholder wealth. Your goals may include the reduction of debt, maintenance of tangible assets (*real* property—real estate and improvements—and *personal* property such as horses, cars, and clothing), and the building of savings and retirement accounts.

DETERMINE YOUR NET WORTH

What is your net worth? You can establish this amount with a chart that lists your *assets*✦ and your *liabilities*✦. First, write down all your assets: a good estimate of the market value of your home and farm; all cash and savings; any cash value in life insurance policies; surrender values in annuities; the current balance in your retirement accounts that you could withdraw today (less income tax, plus 10 percent); the current market value of stocks, bonds, and mutual funds; the market value of your car(s); and a very conservative estimate of household goods. Don't include any personal or family items that you would not be able to sell—you don't want to overstate your assets. Then, list all your liabilities, which are loans or obligations of any type that may include the balance due on a mortgage, car loans, credit card debt, and home equity loans.

Your assets minus your liabilities is your net worth.

A *balance sheet* gives a picture of your net worth on a fixed date in time (fig. 2.1). In a proper balance sheet, accountants use the equation: *assets = liabilities + equity*[+]. ("Equity" is often referred to as "net worth.") The left side of the balance sheet represents your assets and the right side your liabilities and net worth. The total assets should equal liabilities plus net worth.

Determining what your personal balance sheet looks like can help you put your goals into perspective. If you have a negative net worth, start taking steps to improve your balance sheet. Common solutions include reducing debt load or increasing assets.

ALLISON SMITH
BALANCE SHEET AS OF JANUARY 18, 2004

Assets:		Liabilities:	
Home/farm	$450,000	Balance on mortgage	$300,000
Cash, Certificates of Deposit (CDs)	10,000	Balance on auto loans	20,000
Equity in pension plan	25,000	Student loans	10,000
Stocks	5,000	Home equity loans	75,000
Bonds	50,000	Credit lines	8,000
Cars	40,000	Credit card debt	18,000
Horse trailer	10,000	**Total liabilities**	**$431,000**
Household	100,000		
Total assets	**$690,000**		
		Net worth ("equity")	**$259,000**
		Total liabilities plus net worth	**$690,000**

2.1

You can determine where your money comes from, and where it goes over a period of time by using a budget, an important tool for controlling expenses and realizing what areas of spending need to be curbed or increased, depending on your goals.

Your ability to manage cash (called *cash flow*) goes hand-in-hand with a good budget. *Liquidity* (the conversion of assets to cash through sale or exchange—a *liquid* asset is one that is easily converted) is extremely important to solvency; you need to gauge and time your cash flow so your debt obligations are met. You can have plenty of assets on your balance sheet, but if they are not liquid, they are not available at that time and you can end up falling behind on your payments, in foreclosure, or filing bankruptcy.

FINANCIAL RISK MANAGEMENT TOOLS

Brett Alexander Zwerdling, a partner in the firm of Zwerdling and Oppleman in Richmond, Virginia, specializes in bankruptcy. When asked how people end up in bankruptcy, he replies, "It is not so much because of what people do or don't do, it is a matter of circumstance."

You can't always control the circumstances that can leave you vulnerable: these may include becoming unemployed, suffering a disability, or losing a spouse and corresponding income. Other factors, such as inflation and economic problems—both within the United States and globally—can have a profound impact on your financial situation. There are tools you can use to guard against financial upset, however. The most common are:

> Safety nets
> Budgeting and cash flow management
> Debt management
> Credit management
> Organizing your information
> Insurance

In the pages that follow, I will illustrate how you can learn to use all of these.

Safety Nets

Often, a corporation obtains lines of credit to use in the event of a cash flow shortage and only borrows under them if absolutely necessary. You can have similar "safety nets" in place to help cover your household finances: for example, cash to cover three months worth (or more) of your average monthly expenses in interest-bearing savings accounts; certificates of deposit; or other easily liquefiable assets. If having large sums in savings is not feasible, maintain a credit card with a zero balance to use in the event of an emergency. A home equity line of credit (see p. 34) can be used for the same purpose, but again, it is very important not to utilize the credit line until the need arises.

Budgeting and Cash Flow Management

Develop a Budget

Creating an annual *realistic* budget is hard, especially if you have horses. A budget is easily done on paper or with spreadsheet software (though I find that software budget calculators, or those found online, don't offer enough categories, nor include horse-related items). First, use the following five steps to find your *average total monthly expenditures*—the figure upon which you will base your budget (fig. 2.2).

1) Sit down with your checkbook and credit card statements.

2) List your expenditures from the previous twelve months by category. Some categories that may apply to you:

> Automobile maintenance (service, new tires, oil changes)
> Automobile insurance
> Automobile loans
> Federal, state, and local taxes not withheld
> Mortgage payments
> Home equity loans
> Groceries/household items
> Gas
> Electricity
> Fuel/wood for heat
> Water and utilities
> Telephone
> Cell phone
> Clothing/dry cleaning

Personal care (haircuts, etc.)

Recreation and entertainment

Vacation

Spending money and lunches

School and sports activities for children

Farrier

Veterinarian expenses for all animals

Medications for domestic animals (flea and tick control, heartworm preventive, etc.)

Wormer, fly spray, ointments

Boarding fees

Hay

Grain and supplies

Bedding

Horse shows and related attire

Riding instruction

Training clinics

Pasture management (lime, fertilizer, seed)

Credit card payments

Uninsured medical and dental expenses, co-pays and prescriptions

Health insurance

Life insurance

Disability insurance

Horse owner's liability insurance

Retirement funds

Investment funds

Christmas gifts, birthday gifts

3) Then, go through your checkbook and credit card statements and list the relevant monthly expenditures made over the last year in each category. (Items that do not need to be paid for within the next year should not be included. However, if there are purchases that you

Total Average Monthly Expenditure Worksheet
for Two Categories

Grain & Supplies		Groceries & Household Items	
Jan	$155	Jan	$400
Feb	140	Feb	600
Mar	120	Mar	350
Apr	105	Apr	375
May	95	May	450
June	90	June	400
July	90	July	500
Aug	110	Aug	600
Sept	130	Sept	500
Oct	135	Oct	550
Nov	135	Nov	450
Dec	140	Dec	400
Total	**$1,445**	**Total**	**$5,575**
Avg. monthly expenditure:	$120	Avg. monthly expenditure:	$465

Total avg. monthly expenditure (for these two categories): $120 + $465 = $585

2.2

know you will be making later in the year, such as new tires, include the appropriate amount in your yearly automobile maintenance figure, or list it as a separate item.) When you are done, each category should have 12 numbers, an amount for each month.

4) In the first category, add the 12 numbers, and then divide by 12. The resulting figure is your *average monthly expenditure* for that category. Repeat this step for the remaining categories.

5) Finally, add all the average monthly expenditures together. The resulting figure is your *total average monthly expenditure.*

Next, determine your average monthly income, which may include take-home pay, dividends, and interest. Don't include bonuses or overtime in this figure unless they are guaranteed.

MONTHLY BUDGET WORKSHEET

Item	Budgeted	Actual	Difference
Automobile maintenance	$30	$68	- $38
* New tires	71	71	0
* Automobile insurance	150	150	0
Automobile loans	210	210	0
* Taxes not withheld	50	50	0
Mortgage	1,756	1,756	0
Groceries/household items	500	750	- 250
Gas	120	156	- 36
Electricity	175	230	- 55
Telephone	50	50	0
Cell phone	45	62	- 17
Clothing/dry cleaning	100	37	+ 63
Personal care	50	40	+ 10
* Vacation	165	165	0
Farrier	150	150	0
* Veterinarian—all animals	100	100	0
* Medications—animal	90	90	0
Wormer, flyspray, ointments	50	45	+ 5
* Hay	75	75	0
Grain & supplies	120	112	+ 8
Bedding	75	68	+ 7
Riding instruction	160	200	- 40
Savings/investment	100	100	0
Monthy total	**$4,392**	**$4,735**	**- $343**

* Denotes amounts set aside for FUTURE payments on items.
These amounts will be deposited into a special bill paying account.

2.3   The household depicted here owns a farm and two horses. This month, it is about $350 over budget. It needs to *increase* the amount budgeted toward utilities, and *decrease* household and grocery expenditures.

Compare the expenditure and monthly income figures. If expenditures are greater than income, either reduce expenses or increase income. If income is greater than expenditures, then increase savings, retirement plans, and investments.

One way to track expenses in a specific category is to print or copy twelve monthly budget sheets (one for each month), and at the end of each month, record the *actual* amounts spent. Comparing your budgeted figures to the actual numbers helps you gauge how realistic and attainable your budget is. There is room for improvement in any category where expenditures exceed budgeted amounts. (See fig. 2.3 for an example of a monthly budget worksheet.)

Managing Cash Flow

Unfortunately, coming up with a workable budget does not help you manage your cash flow. For this, it's practical to draw up a *cash requirement worksheet* (figs. 2.4 A–C). With this worksheet, you can create a separate, special bill-paying account (either checking or savings) to put aside cash for items that become due *quarterly, semi-annually,* or *annually* and ensure you have enough money to cover those larger bills. Think of your special bill-paying account as an *escrow*✦ account for your future obligations.

The cash requirement worksheet is a simple tool that can be designed with spreadsheet software, or simply drawn on paper. The amount saved monthly toward payment of a bill is entered and then crossed out when the bill is paid. The amount in your special bill-paying account should equal the total sum of the columns on this worksheet.

The cash requirement worksheet is just one element in your overall cash-management system. A simple operating *cash flow statement* helps you see the "big picture" where your money is concerned. See fig. 2.5 for a cash flow statement showing the months of January, February, and March for this household. (Blank monthly budget and cash flow requirement worksheets are available in the *Appendix* for you to use.) The special bill-paying account outlined in figs. 2.4 A–C is listed as a "cash account" on the statement of cash flow.

CASH REQUIREMENT WORKSHEET—FEBRUARY 28, 2005

Item	New Tires	Auto Insurance	Taxes not Withheld	Vacation	Veterinarian	Animal Medications	Hay
Amount	$850	$450 each qtr	varies	$1,950	$1,200	$1,080	$900
Due date	12/31	3/15, 6/15 9/15, 12/15	4/15	1/23/06	throughout year	throughout year	9/15
Save	**$71/mo.**	**$150/mo.**	**$50/mo.**	**$165/mo.**	**$100/mo.**	**$90/mo.**	**$75/mo.**
Balance forward	0	0	400	0	0	0	225
Jan	71	150	50	165	100	90	75
Feb	71	150	50	165	100	90	75
March							
April							
May							
June							
July							
Aug							
Sept							
Oct							
Nov							
Dec	——	——	——	——	——	——	——
Total left for item	**$142**	**$300**	**$500**	**$330**	**$200**	**$180**	**$375**

Total in the bill-paying account as of February 28th: $2,027

2.4 A   **Explanation of items on worksheet:**

- *New tires* costing $850 will be purchased at the end of 2005. Saving $71 per month will reach that goal. ($850 ÷ 12 = $70.83)
- *Automobile insurance* premiums totaling $1,800 annually are paid in $450 quarterly installments. $150 set aside per month is required. ($1,800 ÷ 12 = $150)
- *Taxes* of approximately $600 are due April 15th. ($600 ÷ 12 = $50)
- *Vacation* next January will cost approximately $1,950. A monthly savings of $165 should cover it. ($1,950 ÷ 12 = $162.50)
- *Veterinary costs* for this household's two horses average $1,200 per year. ($1200 ÷ 12 = $100)
- *Animal medications* cost approximately $1,080 per year. ($1,080 ÷ 12 = $90)
- *Hay consumption* averages $900. This household purchases hay in September. ($900 ÷ 12 = $75)

Debt Management

According to the Federal Reserve (the Fed), the total amount of debt owed by consumers in the United States (credit card debt, car and personal loans—but not mortgages) has doubled in the last ten years, and toward the end of 2003 reached $2 trillion. At the same time, the nation's savings rate has gone down considerably.

CASH REQUIREMENT WORKSHEET—MARCH 31, 2005

Item	New Tires	Auto Insurance	Taxes not Withheld	Vacation	Veterinarian	Animal Medications	Hay
Amount	$850	$450 each qtr	varies	$1,950	$1,200	$1,080	$900
Due date	12/31	3/15,6/15 9/15, 12/15	4/15	1/23/06	throughout year	throughout year	9/15
Save	$71/mo.	$150/mo.	$50/mo.	$165/mo.	$100/mo.	$90/mo.	$75/mo.
Balance forward	0	0	400	0	0	0	225
Jan	71	~~150~~	50	165	~~100~~	~~90~~	75
Feb	71	~~150~~	50	165	100	~~90~~	75
March	71	~~150~~	50	165	100	90	75
April							
May							
June							
July							
Aug							
Sept							
Oct							
Nov							
Dec	—	—	—	—	—	—	—
Total left for item	$213	$0	$550	$495	$200	$90	$450

Total in the bill-paying account as of March 31st: **$1,998**

2.4 B **Explanation of items on worksheet:**

Paid during the month of March: a $450 quarterly automobile insurance payment; the veterinarian ($100 for shots); and $180 worth of pet medications. The total of this household's special bill-paying account at the end of March should be $1,998.

The Effect of Interest Rates

During 2003, the Federal Reserve reduced the benchmark *federal funds rate*◆ to the lowest level in over 45 years. As of December 2003, the funds rate was 1 percent, which many hoped to mean the continuance of lower interest rates on many types of loans for consumers and businesses. However, during 2004, the Fed started to tweak rates upward. Why? Because of a change in the demand for money. And, it seems forecasters and analysts

CASH REQUIREMENT WORKSHEET—APRIL 30, 2005

Item	New Tires	Auto Insurance	Taxes not withheld	Vacation	Veterinarian	Animal Medications	Hay
Amount	$850	$450 each qtr	varies	$1,950	$1,200	$1,080	$900
Due date	12/31	3/15, 6/15 9/15, 12/15	4/15	1/23/06	throughout year	throughout year	9/15
Save	$71/mo.	$150/mo.	$50/mo.	$165/mo.	$100/mo.	$90/mo.	$75/mo.
Balance forward	0	0	400	0	0	0	225
Jan	71	150	50	165	100	90	75
Feb	71	150	50	165	100	90	75
March	71	150	50	165	100	90	75
April	71	150	50	165	100	90	75
May							
June							
July							
Aug							
Sept							
Oct							
Nov							
Dec	___	___	___	___	___	___	___
Total left for items	$284	$150	$0	$660	$300	$180	$525

Total in the bill-paying account as of April 30th: $2,099

2.4 C   **Explanation of items on worksheet:**

In April, this household paid $600 in taxes. The total in the account at the end of the month should be $2,099.

THREE-MONTH CASH FLOW STATEMENT

	January	February	March
Inflow:			
Salaries	$5,500	$5,500	$5,500
Dividends	100	100	100
Total cash inflow	**$5,600**	**$5,600**	**$5,600**
Outflow (what you *actually* pay out):			
Automobile	$ 434	$ 330	$ 330
Auto insurance	0	0	450
Mortgage	1,756	1,756	1,756
Groceries/household	750	450	528
Utilities	342	270	270
Clothing/dry cleaning	37	50	48
Personal care	40	43	40
Farrier	150	150	150
Veterinarian	0	0	100
Medications	0	0	180
Wormer, etc.	45	45	46
Grain and supplies	112	115	112
Bedding	68	68	68
Riding instruction	200	160	160
Investment—IRA	100	100	100
Other	0	0	0
Total cash outflow	**$4,034**	**$3,537**	**$4,338**
Net cash flow	**$1,566**	**$2,063**	**$1,262**
Beginning balance in cash accounts:			
Regular checking	$1,000	$1,865	$1,227
Savings	2,000	2,000	4,000
Special bill-paying account	625	1,326	2,027
Beginning cash balance	***$3,625**	***$5,191**	***$7,254**
Ending balance in cash accounts:			
Regular checking	$1,865	$1,227	$1,518
Savings	2,000	4,000	5,000
Special bill paying-account	1,326	2,027	1,998
Ending cash balance	***$5,191**	***$7,254**	***$8,516**

*Please note that the ending cash balance for January becomes the beginning cash balance for February, and so on.

2.5

PRIME RATE FLUCTUATIONS

The economy is cyclical in nature. For example, during the Great Depression years (1933–1935), the *prime rate*✦ was approximately 1.5 percent. Below are some random time frames that show the fluctuation in the prime rate, according to the Federal Reserve:

1933–1935	1.5%
August 1956	4%
June 1969	8.5%
July 1974	12%
December 1976	6.25%
April 1980	20%
July 1981	20.5%
February 1989	11.5%
November 2001	5%
February 2005	5.5%

These months represent highs and lows over the years. Between them, there were fluctuations. Rates steadily declined from 2001 until 2004, when it averaged 4 percent.

are divided as to whether the economy may face a significant increase in inflation in 2006 and beyond. Further, there is a large federal budget deficit that appears as though it will continue to increase in the years to come. A budget deficit is a sign of instability in both individual business and government. It is viewed as a credit risk, and riskier borrowers are charged higher interest rates by lenders and investors. The federal deficit, therefore, sets the stage for future increases in interest rates.

SO YOU KNOW...

✦ The *prime rate* is the interest rate banks charge their best (preferred) customers. Changes in the prime rate influence other rates, including mortgage rates.

As interest rates again rise, households that have considerable consumer debt may very well be stressed. Their debt burden will increase and continue to grow as loans with *variable interest* (credit card loans, for example) cost more.

Refinancing Your Mortgage

When 30-year mortgage rates are low (as they are at the time of writing), you should consider *refinancing* to "lock into" the lower rates and reduce your monthly payments. You can also refinance for more than the balance on your first mortgage in order to obtain cash to settle other debt, such as credit card loans. The interest on your mortgage is tax deductible, whereas interest on personal and automobile loans, for example, is not.

Refinancing may not be worth the cost for those who have recently obtained a mortgage. Discuss your options with a mortgage broker or loan officer. Items to consider when refinancing include: the interest rate you can obtain with your credit rating (see p. 35); the number of points (each point is 1 percent of the amount of the loan) the lender would charge; the mortgage fees and other costs associated with refinancing; how long you plan on keeping the house; and the tax effect.

Home Equity Loans

A fixed-rate *home equity loan*✦ is a way to consolidate your bills and lower your interest costs by paying off high-interest credit cards and car loans. The interest on the home equity loan may be tax deductible providing you have not mortgaged over 100 percent of your home's market value. (Consult your tax advisor before obtaining a home equity loan, as other constraints may apply and the tax code changes frequently.) The major drawback to a home equity loan, or *home equity line*✦, is that the debt is secured by your home, so if your payments fall behind, you could lose your house. Remember, if you pay off credit cards with your loan or line only to run up balances again, you will find yourself in financial "hot water."

Credit Cards

One way to reduce your interest cost on debt is to transfer credit card balances to a card with a lower, *fixed interest rate*✦. But, be aware that continually switching cards to obtain low, introductory offers may not be beneficial—for several reasons. First, many cards have a *variable interest rate*✦. In such cases, initial low rates "spike" after the introductory period, and you may end up stuck with debt on a card with a higher-than-normal interest rate—not the optimal situation for debt management. Second, lenders don't look favorably on "card hoppers" who haven't established a consistent credit history with a particular lender.

Student Loans

If you have qualified student loans (those used for school-related needs such as housing, books, and tuition), consider *consolidating* them. With consolidation, all the loans taken out each school year are wrapped into one, and you can "lock in" to a low, fixed rate of interest for the life of the loan and extend your payment term, making your monthly payments much smaller. Under most circumstances, interest on student loans is tax deductible. Consult your tax advisor on limits for the deduction concerning adjusted gross income levels and filing status.

Credit Management

Credit Reports

The credit reports that a lender obtains from the three major credit-reporting agencies (see *Resources*, p. 219, for contact information) are used to determine whether or not you qualify for a loan. For example, an insurance company may access your credit information in order to determine which risk category you fall into, and this, in turn, may affect the premiums you pay.

The credit reports detail how much you have borrowed and how much you owe. They also reveal bad credit, such as missed and late payments, repossessions, and delinquent accounts. This information remains in your history for seven years. (Bankruptcy can remain on your credit report for ten years.) Your credit history determines your credit rating or "score"—a credit score of 600 points is average, 700 is good, and 800 is excellent. Every time a credit-reporting agency receives an inquiry from a lender—this happens when you apply for a credit card or loan—your credit score can be negatively affected because each time your report is accessed, points are deducted.

It is of the utmost importance to your long-term financial health to maintain a good credit report. If your credit history is less than stellar, start today and make sure all your payments are on time and in accordance with the creditor's agreement. At least once a year, you should obtain copies of your credit reports from the major credit-reporting agencies to check for inaccuracy and guard against identity theft.

Keep Track of Accounts

Be diligent in your record-keeping and reconcile bank statements regularly. Most banks have telephone or online banking access so you can make sure your debt payments have cleared your bank in the correct amount and in a timely fashion. Creditors, and even financial institutions, can (and do) make mistakes. Suppose, for example, your monthly minimum payment for your credit card is $50, and you write a check for $100—but the lender erroneously records only $10 on the deposit slip. The check then clears for an insufficient amount, and you are delinquent in the eyes of the creditor (even though the check you wrote more than covered the bill). A quick call to the lender will save you late charges tacked on to your account, not to mention a big hassle if the delinquency is reported to the credit agencies.

Fraud is another motive to check accounts and statements. If someone has accessed your checking account number and printed checks, or stolen your ATM card and access identification numbers, "red flags"— such as unidentifiable purchases or withdrawals in states you haven't visited—will show up on your bank statement. Also look over your credit card statements to be certain all charges are correct.

Beware Automatic Default Language

Many credit card companies have changed their "terms of agreement" to include a clause that states if you are late with a payment on a different account with them, or another credit card provider, or any other creditor, you are automatically deemed *in default* and your interest rate jumps to 19.99 percent—or higher. This means that if you are even one day late paying a telephone bill and it is transmitted to the credit-reporting agencies, you are in default on all your credit cards. You usually receive these change-of-terms notices with your monthly statement.

Organizing Your Information

Keeping personal and financial information organized can be difficult in the world we live in. However, it is important that you take the time as "knowing where everything is" will help you manage your cash flow more efficiently and avoid potential financial pitfalls. Once you get a filing system set up, maintaining information is relatively easy.

Critical Items

A "fireproof" box at home, and/or safe-deposit box at your local bank, will help keep your personal and financial information safe. It is important to note that fireproof boxes can only withstand heat and flame for a specified amount of time, and therefore, you may prefer to keep certain items of importance at the bank. With that in mind, I suggest the following items be stored in a safe manner:

> Deeds
>
> Wills
>
> Titles to vehicles
>
> Copies of your mortgages, loans, and notes
>
> Investment records
>
> Retirement and social security statements
>
> Employment benefit information
>
> Copy of your current health insurance information
>
> Homeowner's, liability, and automobile insurance policies
>
> Seven years worth of tax returns and supporting documentation
>
> Marriage certificates and identification records
>
> Court orders for divorce, child support
>
> *Current* credit card statements and bank statements
>
> Registration papers for horses and other pets

Also, keep proof of payment of any child support, spousal support, and/or alimony in your fireproof box or safe-deposit box. My business law professor likes to share a story about one of his clients whose ex-wife was supposed to receive support for twenty years pursuant to their divorce, and the man dutifully made every payment. Nonetheless, at the end of the term, the client was served notice that his ex-wife was taking him to court, claiming non-payment of the entire amount! Burden of proof is on the defendant, and if the man could not prove he had made those payments, he could have been found liable to pay them again. As my professor tells it, his client walked into his office with shoe boxes full of cancelled checks—all twenty years worth—set them on his lawyer's desk and said, "I know this woman."

The moral? Permanently keep all payment records for anything to do with a court order or loans from a private lender.

Basic Items

Bills

You don't necessarily have to put basic monthly bills (both paid and unpaid), such as utility, electric, phone, and cable, in a safe. However, tell somebody where these bills are in the event something happens to you. It is also a good idea to write down bills that are due—amounts, terms, and payment addresses of creditors—as someone assisting you may not have knowledge of mortgage payments, or other debts, that are automatically deducted from your checking account or that do not generate mailed monthly statements (a payment booklet, for example).

Proof of Purchase

Organize your receipts. Keep purchase receipts in a folder or large envelope labeled by year. Proof of important purchases, such as diamonds, vehicles, or other big-ticket items, should be in a safe. You may need to produce them in the event of an insurance claim. Take pictures of your property, buildings, and each room in your house and store them in a safe-deposit box away from your residence. Photographs can help you itemize your losses in the event your home is destroyed by fire. Add lists of items in each room, as well.

Equine and Pet Information

Equine and other pet information should also be organized and easily found in the event of your unexpected absence or illness. If you board your horse, be sure that the owner and manager of the boarding barn has an informed contact to reach who can make decisions or take action on your behalf. Provide written instructions for feeding, worming, turnout, farrier, large animal veterinarian, vaccinations, medications, supplements, and special needs—especially if you have your horses on your own property.

Make up information sheets for all other pets, as well. Include your small animal vet and pet sitter's names, addresses, and phone numbers. Nominate a person who knows your horses and pets, and who is willing to efficiently and competently care for them in your absence.

How Long to Keep Information

How long should you keep important information? This will vary, depending on the item under consideration. Generally, for an individual, tax records and all supporting documentation should be kept for seven years. However, the Internal Revenue Service (IRS) has no time limitation if you ever failed to file a return or filed a fraudulent return. Individual Retirement Account (IRA) contributions, retirement and savings plan statements, and bank records should be kept permanently.

Hold on to brokerage statements until seven years after the securities have been sold and you have filed the subsequent tax returns. It is a good idea to keep credit card statements until the account is closed and reported to the credit bureaus as closed by the consumer. (You only need to keep *current* statements in a fireproof box.)

Each year, match your paycheck stubs to the W-2 forms from your employer, and if everything is correct, you can throw the stubs away. W-2s can be thrown away after seven years.

Receipts for improvements or remodeling your premises should be kept until seven years after the home/farm is sold. These costs are added to your *cost basis*✦ in determining capital gains upon the sale of the property (see p. 138).

> ═ SO YOU KNOW... ═
>
> ✦ *Cost basis* or *basis* is a tax term for an asset's purchase price plus the commissions and expenses necessary to make the asset usable, or to improve it.

Insurance

An insurance policy is a contract between you and an insurance company wherein you pay a *premium* (a fixed amount that is paid, usually per month), and in exchange, the company promises to pay for specifically named losses in the event they should occur. It is financially responsible to insure your household in several different areas; I have outlined some of them on the following pages.

Life Insurance

A life insurance policy is important for managing personal risk. For instance, if you die and your household is negatively affected by the loss of income, your spouse and dependents, including animals, will be cared for. Ideally, you would want your spouse to be able to pay the mortgage, household bills, invest for retirement, and maintain a lifestyle close to what he or she currently enjoys. Life insurance can also provide benefits during your lifetime—some policies are designed to help you finance your retirement or a child's education through *cash value*✦ build up.

There are two types of life insurance policies—*term* and *whole life* (cash value insurance).

Term

Term insurance is a pure insurance wherein the owner pays an annual premium for the policy and no cash value accrues. If the insured dies during that year, his designated beneficiaries receive the face amount, also called the "stated value," of the policy. (This is similar to car and homeowner's insurance.) The older you are, the more expensive term insurance is to buy; however, some companies offer what is called *level term* insurance, where the premiums remain the same for a stated number of years—5, 10, 15, or 30—so you know how much you'll have to pay in the future.

Whole Life

The other type of life insurance policy is a *whole life* contract. This is paid for over a specified number of years and covers the insured for his entire life. A portion of the annual premium is invested by the insurance company, and the policy owner receives a modest portion of any interest, which builds cash value in the policy over time. This cash value can often be used—either in the form of a loan or withdrawal—by the insured during his lifetime, should the need arise.

Since all life insurance policies are based on age, health, and similar factors, the younger and healthier the insured at the beginning of the contract, the cheaper the insurance premiums. Annual premiums for whole life cost more than term insurance. For this reason, term insurance is popular with young couples starting out.

The dollar amount of life insurance you need to carry depends on a variety of factors. If your goal is debt coverage, all borrowings, including your mortgage, car loan, and any unsecured debt owed, need to be considered. The appropriate policy value for estate-planning purposes, on the other hand, depends on the size of the estate and the tax laws in effect at the time of your death—if your estate is sizeable, your heirs could use the life insurance proceeds to pay federal estate taxes. Speak to a life and health agent licensed in your state about what might be best for your particular situation.

Disability Insurance

Disability coverage—often offered by your employer's benefits package—pays you a monthly amount in the event you become disabled. The benefits are based on a percentage of your income and are usually paid to age 65, when you receive Social Security and retirement benefits. In order to compare policies, some clauses you should be aware of include, but are not limited to:

- *Elimination period*—the time you have to wait for coverage to begin after becoming disabled.

- *Definition of disabled*—you need the policy to consider you are disabled when you can no longer perform your *own* occupation, i.e. the work you normally do. If the policy has a much broader definition of disability, this reduces your benefits.

- *Maximum benefit allowed under the life of the policy*—the dollar limit of coverage.

- *Tax consequences of paying premiums with before-tax or after-tax income*—the general rule is if you pay with after-tax income, the benefits are income-tax free, and if you pay premiums with before-tax dollars, the benefits are taxable when paid.

Health Insurance

Health insurance is also frequently part of your employer's benefits package. If you are self-employed or do not have health insurance coverage, you should consult an agent to help you locate the best policy for an affordable price, as uninsured medical expenses can be financially devastating.

There are two basic types of health care coverage, *traditional* and *managed care. Traditional* insurance plans allow you to go to a provider (i.e., hospital or physician) of your choice, but you are required to pay up front for the services and file claims for reimbursement (though some plans allow the hospital or doctor to file for compensation directly from the insurer). *Managed care* health insurance uses a network of selected doctors and other providers with whom the insurance company has arranged the amounts to be charged for certain services. You usually pay more for a traditional than a managed care health insurance policy.

MAKE SURE COVERED CLAIMS GET PAID

Unfortunately, many of you will need to utilize your health insurance for surgery or another involved claim. And sometimes, a doctor or hospital, through coding or processing error charges you for items that *are* covered under your insurance plan. When this happens and you contact the insurance company or doctor's office only to hear the words, "We will take care of it," don't assume it will be done!

Often, this bill gets sent to a collections agency before you realize it, and then the "delinquent" account gets reported to the credit bureaus, ending up on your credit report. Sometimes, it can take months to get a claim resolved. So, always make sure bills have been settled and obtain written confirmation that the matter is resolved. If a delinquency was incorrectly reported to the credit bureau, make sure it is completely removed from your credit report and notated as an *error*—not a delinquent account that was finally paid.

Long-Term Care Insurance

When preparing for the future, the importance of planning to pay for *long-term care* is often forgotten or ignored. This can be financially draining—even devastating—because annual costs in a skilled nursing facility can run well over $50,000. (Rates vary widely by state: the American Association of Retired Persons—or AARP—has information about average costs for nursing home care state by state.) Purchasing a long-term care insurance policy helps to minimize the risk of having too little money to pay someone to care for you when you can no longer care for yourself. This policy allows you to plan in advance and fund associated expenses.

When considering such a policy, a few items to discuss with your licensed life and health insurance agent include:

- *Maximum benefits allowed under the policy*—the dollar limit of coverage.

- *Elimination period*—the waiting time for benefits to start.

- *Covered services*—what is included and excluded under the policy.

- *Benefit triggers under the policy*—generally, coverage begins when the insured can no longer perform a specific number of daily living activities, such as eating, bathing, or walking.

Property and Casualty Insurance

Property insurance covers your interest in a physical property for its loss or the loss of its income-producing abilities, and *casualty* is just another name for liability—such types of insurance cover your legal liability for injuries done to others, or damages done to another's property. This includes home-, horse-, and business-owner's insurance, automobile insurance, as well as general and commercial liability insurance, to name a few.

Homeowner's Insurance

There are various forms of property coverage. I will limit my discussion to the "fully loaded" homeowner's policy, which provides insurance for your dwelling, personal property, other structures on the premises, and liability. Consult your agent and determine whether the following key items are included in your policy:

- Replacement coverage on your dwelling and personal property.

- Replacement coverage on your barn(s). It is best to list barns as "other structures" rather than underwrite them as a separate endorsement to your policy, which can be more expensive.

- Schedule of artwork, antiques, and jewelry. This is a specific list of items of particular worth insured for their full value, which may be over and above the "jewelry" or "artwork" limit in your policy.

- Liability coverage of your horses both on and off your property.

- Coverage of legal fees should you need to defend yourself.

You should also ask about:

- *Covered perils*, such as fire and wind. Some perils, sewer and septic backup, for example, may have to be added to your policy by endorsement.

- How to ensure all your property has adequate coverage and is represented properly under your policy.

- How to avoid becoming underinsured and keep policy limits current.

Homeowner's insurance saves you from financial loss by providing the means to rebuild structures or reacquire items that may be damaged or destroyed. While quite often nothing can prevent the occurrence of a disaster, you and your household will be able to put the pieces back together far more quickly with the aid this coverage provides.

Automobile Insurance

Automobile insurance provides a method of paying for specific vehicle-related financial losses during the term of your policy. In many states, drivers are required by law to carry *liability coverage* or *no-fault personal injury protection* to pay for losses they may cause others and medical and related expenses due to a car accident. Drivers often elect to also get *collision* and *comprehensive coverage* on their vehicle(s). Collision pays for any damage incurred if you hit another object or roll your car, and comprehensive coverage insures your vehicle in case of vandalism, theft, or breakage caused by fire, wind, flood, or other forces of nature.

If you own a horse trailer, it is important that it is covered for both collision and comprehensive and listed separately on your automobile policy, because when your trailer is attached to a vehicle with liability coverage, it is covered for liability *only*. In this case, if your trailer is hit by another vehicle or a tree falls on it, your insurance will *not* pay for the damages sustained.

Personal Liability Umbrella

In our increasingly litigious society, many individuals provide their personal and financial interests an extra layer of protection by investing in *personal liability umbrella* policies. These offer coverage over and above your other types of insurance, such as your homeowner's or automobile policies. A personal liability umbrella *only* activates when other coverage is exhausted. For example, if you are the cause of a major car accident involving several vehicles and numerous injuries, the damages you are responsible for may go well beyond the limits on your regular automobile policy. In this case, the personal liability umbrella could save you from financial ruin.

More often than not, this type of coverage is relatively inexpensive— and it could be invaluable as a protection for your current assets and future earnings. Those who can especially benefit from personal liability umbrellas include professionals, families with young drivers, owners of rental property, and sports enthusiasts (i.e., horseback riders, skiers, and boaters).

Equine-Specific Insurance

Personal Horse Owner's Liability

Most homeowner's insurance policies do not cover equine-related exposures, so as a horse owner, it is prudent to purchase a *personal horse owner's liability* policy. This policy covers your legal liability for bodily injury and property damage to others caused by your animal, and also any defense costs. Make sure this coverage is provided when the horse is *on* and *off* "owned premises," so if you keep your horse at a boarding stable, you have coverage.

Some insurers have restrictions: the *personal* horse owner's liability policy will not cover exposures resulting from any type of *commercial* activity. This means that if you receive money or any other type of compensation for an equine activity, such as boarding a neighbor's horse or giving riding lessons to a friend, you may jeopardize your coverage. In these cases, you need a *commercial general liability* (CGL) policy. This policy will cover personal horse exposures, as well as those that could be considered "business" exposures. (For more information on CGL policies, see p. 159.)

Regardless of your insurance coverage, it is a good idea to use a *waiver* anytime someone rides your horses or spends time in your barn. "Susie from next door" might not dream of making a claim on your liability policy, but her insurance company could. Consult an attorney about items your waiver should include, and be sure he reviews and revises it for legal adequacy and accuracy.

Equine Mortality / Theft, Loss of Use, and Medical / Surgical Insurance

If the purchase price of your horse was sizeable, and the money for a replacement horse hard to come by, *equine mortality/theft* coverage can be obtained. Many mortality policies offer an *agreed value*⁕ settlement wherein the purchase price of the insured animal is paid upon his death. (This is similar to *term life insurance* for a person, see p. 40.) They can include coverage for humane destruction in the event it becomes necessary due to injury or illness, and insure your horse in case of theft. Mortality policies usually provide guaranteed renewal coverage and extension provisions.

If your horse's value is dependent on his ability to perform a specific function, such as jumping or racing, *loss of use* coverage can added to your equine mortality policy. This is similar to *disability insurance* for a person with an "own occupation" rider on his policy: if a heart surgeon is in a terrible car accident that crushes his hands and he can no longer perform intricate surgical procedures, his disability insurance will pay him a benefit. In the same way, if a horse can no longer perform his intended job, loss of use coverage pays the owner a benefit.

Medical/surgical policies are generally riders or attachments to mortality/theft policies, and offer coverage for veterinary bills and costs associated with a severe injury or illness. They do not cover routine veterinary care and vaccinations, travel expenses, elective surgery, or holistic treatments.

Insurance Overview

When considering insurance companies, it is best to shop around for the best rates and coverage available. Enlist an insurance agent licensed in your state to help you with your search. Make sure the company is financially sound by checking the financial strength ratings with an agency, such as A.M. Best or Standard & Poor's. You can also review a company's "complaint history" filed with your state's department of insurance. Consumer information, guides, and booklets are available through your state and the National Association of Insurance Commissioners (NAIC). Contact information for the NAIC, the National Committee for Quality Assurance (NCQA), and rating agencies for life and long-term care insurance companies, can be found in *Resources*, p. 220.

Contact a property and casualty insurance agent for quotes on a personal horse owner's liability policy with your desired limits of coverage, as well as equine mortality/theft and medical/surgical insurance. Premiums for these types of coverage depend upon the insurer's underwriting guidelines, which may include the breed, age, sex, use, and purchase price of the horse, and your location. I've included information to help you locate equine insurance providers on p. 219.

Finally, read *every* policy thoroughly upon receipt and understand the terms and conditions contained therein. If there is anything that you don't understand, it is important to call the insurer or agent with any questions *before* you have an event that could result in a claim. There are responsibilities the insured—you—must fulfill in order to maintain coverage.

Part II
RETIREMENT, INVESTMENTS, AND TAX PLANNING

RETIREMENT PLANNING

Social Security

Creating your own plan for retirement is prudent, especially if you are now in your twenties or thirties. Unless substantial changes—other than privatization—are made to the system, it appears as though Social Security will not sustain future retirees at the benefit levels we currently expect.

The Social Security Administration estimates that by 2018 it will begin to pay out more than is collected in taxes, and by 2042 it will have exhausted its reserves. The reasons given for this long-range financing problem are that people are living longer and the birth rate is lower: in 2008, 79 million "baby boomers" will begin retiring, and by 2030, there will be nearly twice as many older Americans as there are today, while at the same time, the number of workers paying into Social Security *per beneficiary* will drop from 3.3 to approximately 2.

As a general rule, financial analysts estimate that most people require at least 70 percent of their pre-retirement income in order to live comfortably; however, with today's rising health care costs, 80 to 90 percent is now often required by retirees. Social Security benefits are supposed to replace 40 percent of this and the balance comes from pensions, individual savings, and investments. Because of the looming problems with the Social Security System, it now appears that pensions, savings, and investments may become the mainstay of retirement income (for more information, see *Resources*, p. 220).

Pensions and Savings

As you can see, you need to save for your retirement, and the earlier you start the better. For example, if you invest an initial lump sum of $3,000 in a retirement account that earns interest at a rate of 7.5 percent, compounded annually, and you continue to contribute the same amount each year, in 44 years, your account will reach $1,000,000! And, your actual cash outlay was only about $132,000—this shows the "power" of compound interest and is a good example of the "time value" of money.

Compound interest occurs when interest paid on an investment is added to the principal, so interest is earned on an increasingly larger sum. Interest can be compounded annually, semi-annually, monthly, weekly, or daily. The more compounding periods per year, the more your money will earn.

Obviously, the higher the interest rate, the more your investment will accrue. For example, let's say Allison Smith wants to retire in 35 years with $750,000 in savings. In order to achieve this with an account that earns 6 percent interest annually, she will have to put in approximately $6,730 per year. In this case, her total cash outlay will be around $235,550. However, if her account earns 9 percent interest annually, she will only need to deposit $3,477 each year, and her total cash outlay will be much less—around $121,695.

Employer Sponsored Retirement Plans

If you have a retirement plan, such as a 401(k) through your place of employment, and you are *vested*✦ in that plan, it is wise to make the maximum contributions that your employer will match. Although it often requires additional budget planning to enable you to set aside large amounts of your income, it is worth the effort: usually, the money you contribute is tax-deductible and grows tax-free until it is withdrawn.

Individual Retirement Accounts

If you are eligible, you can open an individual retirement account (IRA) at a financial institution, brokerage firm, or directly with a mutual fund. The amount you can contribute, and subsequently deduct, for a traditional IRA depends on various factors, such as your age, filing status, and modified adjusted gross income. For 2005, if you are under the age of 50, the maximum contribution to an IRA is $4,000 for a single contribution or $8,000 for a combined contribution (i.e.,

SO YOU KNOW...

✦ *Vested* benefits are guaranteed to an employee, even if the employee leaves the company. Usually, pension benefits are based on contributions from both the employee and the company. If the employee resigns, he only keeps the portion he contributed. However, after working at a company for a designated period of time, the employee also keeps the contribution the employer makes—the benefits are *vested*.

you and your spouse). If you are 50 or older, the maximum single contribution is $4,500—or $9,000 combined.

There are two types of IRAs, the *Traditional* and the *Roth*. The Internal Revenue Service (IRS) gives you a tax break on both. With a *Traditional*, the tax break is up front: you can use your contributions as a tax deduction. However, when you retire and start drawing money out of the account, it will be taxed as income. There are also rules about receiving the *distributions*◆: you are penalized for early withdrawals, and you must begin receiving required minimum amounts by April 1 of the year following the year you reach 70½. When you begin receiving the required withdrawals, you can no longer make contributions.

Roth IRAs allow you to contribute to the account using "take-home" pay, and the interest earned on your investment is not taxed as income when you retire and receive distributions—as long as you satisfy all the IRS requirements. Contributions can be made to a Roth IRA regardless of your age, you can leave amounts in the account as long as you want, and upon your death, your beneficiaries may receive distributions income-tax-free. The IRS does impose limits on the amount you can contribute, depending on various factors such as your filing status and modified adjusted gross income.

A Traditional IRA allows withdrawals to be taxed at the same rate as ordinary income, so a huge chunk of your retirement money goes to the government, whereas with a Roth IRA, it stays in your account. Inflation and tax rates are out of your control, but by using a Roth IRA, you may only need to deal with inflation and its effects on your money when you reach retirement age. Roth IRAs are a good deal, especially if you are not close to retirement. (If retirement is 30 or 40 years away, you can't predict whether tax rates will be higher or lower than they are now.)

IRS Publication 590, *Individual Retirement Arrangements*, contains the complete guidelines for IRAs and is available online (see *Resources*, p. 220). You should obtain a copy of the updated publication each year as guidelines may change.

Investments

Fixed Income Investments
Fixed income investments are securities that pay a fixed rate of return. You

can buy government, corporate, or municipal bonds, which pay you a fixed rate of interest on the money you lend until they mature, or *preferred stock* (which pays a fixed dividend), *certificates of deposit (CDs),* or *guaranteed interest contracts (GICs).*

Bonds are advantageous when interest rates are low. However, as interest rates increase, existing bonds decrease in value. Regardless, the bond market remains attractive to investors because of the stability bonds can provide to an investment portfolio. And, diversification within a bond portfolio can be done by purchasing bonds that vary by date of maturity, quality, yield and by investing in a number of different issues.

Equity Investments◆

Stocks

Stocks represent shares of ownership in a company; when you invest in a stock, you as a "shareholder" possess an ownership interest in a corporation by virtue of owning their stock. Analysts recommend buying stock when the market is low and selling when it is high.

The stock market should be considered an investment for long-term holding—over time, the returns can be higher than with other types of investments. However, it is volatile—the timing of the market swings or the performance of individual stocks cannot be predicted. People's retirement plans or invested funds can be devastated by the market's performance. Choose a stock portfolio with the help of a qualified investment analyst, diversify, and utilize bonds to provide stability.

Real Estate

Real estate is another equity investment. A substantial total return after its sale, plus the ability to purchase rental property, borrow money in the form of a mortgage against that property, and collect rent and make a profit (called *leverage*), are two advantages. Real estate is also considered a good *hedge* (or protection) against inflation, because property values and rents tend to increase during inflationary times. There are tax advantages, as well, to owning real estate.

Some disadvantages include the need for a large initial investment; the cost of maintaining the property during ownership; the expenses associated with buying, selling, or renting; and the risk of the property losing market appeal.

SO YOU KNOW...

◆ An *equity investment* represents an ownership interest.

Mutual Funds

Mutual funds are managed by investment companies that pool money raised from you—and thousands of others—and invest it in stocks, bonds, options, and money market securities. These funds offer the individual investor—who becomes a shareholder in the fund—the advantage of diversification and professional management. They are usually very liquid investments and most will redeem existing shares on demand (i.e. will buy your shares back from you when you need to sell.)

There is a management fee—usually a percentage of your annual investment. In addition to this fee, you often pay commission (known as "loads") when you purchase or sell shares of the fund. Usually, a "no-load" fund does not charge a sales commission, therefore your transactions occur at the mutual fund's *net-asset value* (market price) per share.

The net-asset value of the mutual fund's shares fluctuates daily with the market prices of the holdings that make up its portfolio. A mutual fund's objectives can range from high-yield (generally aggressive, riskier investments) to the lower, steady yield of conservative investments. (A fund's management objectives and investment policies are described in its prospectus, which is often available online.) There are funds to meet almost any investment goal—some only invest in bonds, others in stocks, and even others in hybrid funds, which invest in stocks, bonds, and money market instruments. Evaluate and assess your risk tolerance before buying shares in a fund.

Diversify for Risk Management

Diversification among quality investments is the key to a stable portfolio that gives you a steady return. Spread your risk by owning different types of investments, limiting your exposure to a particular investment sector, and having many different *obligors* (entities that issue stocks and/or bonds).

In the case of mutual funds, their appeal is the diversification and management expertise they offer; however, if possible, own shares in more than one—diversity among mutual funds is beneficial, because even though a fund may invest in a variety of instruments, you own shares of just one entity. With investments, always heed the old saying, "Don't put all your eggs in one basket."

Tax Planning

For tax planning purposes, the use of qualified retirement plans and IRAs allows you to build up tax-deferred wealth. Interest on United States savings bonds is exempt from state and local taxes and no federal tax is due until the bonds are redeemed. A municipal bond, which is a debt obligation of a state or local municipality, is for the most part, tax exempt. Usually, a bondholder will not have to pay federal income tax on the interest and does not have to pay state taxes if the bond was issued in his or her state of residence; however, some bonds—though exempt from federal taxation—are taxed on the state level. The more complicated your investment portfolio and finances, the more valuable a certified public accountant will become.

When considering a transaction, the possibility of saving on taxes should be an important consideration, but not to the exclusion of other factors. A transaction will not be recognized for tax purposes unless it is economically feasible in other regards—in other words, you can't enter into a deal just to save on your taxes. Carefully consider the possible loss of flexibility in your funds when making long-term financial commitments for tax-savings purposes. Tax laws change regularly, thereby making imperative the need for tax planning assistance from a qualified professional.

Donating a Horse as a Charitable Contribution

If you wish to donate a horse to a riding school or a therapeutic riding center, you can use the gift as a tax deduction: a non-cash charitable contribution to a qualified (IRS recognized) organization. Usually, the amount of a charitable contribution is the fair market value of the property at the time of contribution, as most property decreases in value over time. Even if the horse you are donating is worth more than what you paid for him, however, your charitable deduction will be limited to his purchase value (cost basis).

Any "contribution" over $500, but under $5,000, requires a written record outlining how you obtained the horse, the date you assumed ownership, and documentation of your cost basis. If your horse is worth over $5,000, you will need a professional appraisal, in addition. Obtain a written acknowledgement of the contribution from the recipient.

Part III
WILLS AND ESTATE PLANNING

WILLS

General Wills

Most people don't like to think about dying, however, preparing a *will* that specifies how you want your estate handled and assets distributed is essential. A will names your executor (the individual designated to administer your estate), and can be used to set up trusts for your children or animals, and, if they are still minors, appoint a guardian for your children. It does not take effect until you pass away and can be changed or revoked at any time before. If you don't have a will, each state has laws on descent and distribution that guide how an estate is handled.

There are costs associated with settling an estate (ask a local attorney for an estimate of the fees required for an estate the size of yours). All states require them to be paid out of the estate funds. *Probate*—the court's recognition of a will as valid and enforceable—involves identifying the deceased's property subject to probate (assets in your name only, for example), valuing the assets through appraisal, and then paying taxes and creditors on behalf of the deceased. The estate's administrator is responsible for filing the required income, inheritance, and/or estate tax returns, as well as an account of his handling of the estate. (If you have a will, your named executor will act as your administrator, if not, the court will appoint someone.)

> **SO YOU KNOW...**
> ✦ Your *probate estate* is the property that is handled and distributed by your executor or administrator.

Most jurisdictions require that the executor post a bond to protect the assets of the estate until they can be distributed to the creditors, heirs, and benefactors of the will. Any real estate or personal property owned jointly with right of survivorship will pass to the surviving parties. Life insurance proceeds, and balances in IRAs and other retirement plans pass to the named beneficiaries and are not subject to probate.

A will can ensure that should something happen to you, your horse will be provided for. Given the lifespan of some horses, it is possible that the six-year-old gelding you purchased when you were 55 will outlive you. According to Jeffrey M. Zwerdling, Esq., a principal in the law firm of Zwerdling and Oppleman in Richmond, Virginia, horses and livestock are considered chattel or personal property under Virginia law and, therefore, can be devised (transferred or "gifted") through a will. This is true in most states. If you have someone who has agreed to take care of your horse, you can specify this in the will and also bequeath a sum of money to cover the costs involved.

It is possible, of course, to create and type your own will—computer software is available, if needed—but in order for it to be a valid and enforceable document, it must be executed in accordance with the legal requirements of your state. When discussing wills, Mr. Zwerdling cautions, "If you don't know how to ride a horse and you jump on and go galloping off, chances are you are going to get hurt. The same is true for using legal forms…you must understand the legal implications of them in order not to get yourself in trouble."

I advise getting an attorney's input. It is worth the expense—for an estate worth less than $1.5 million, an attorney would charge between $400 and $700 for husband and wife wills of medium complexity.

Living Wills

A *living will* goes into effect only when you become terminally ill and are unable to act on your own behalf. For example, you can direct your physician to withdraw life support when you are in an irreversible coma or vegetative state, or stipulate your wishes concerning resuscitation, artificial nutrition, and comfort measures, such as pain medication and oxygen therapy. Obtain legal advice regarding the wording of your living will to be certain it conforms to your state's laws.

ESTATE TAXES—A BRIEF OVERVIEW

The *federal estate tax* is a transfer tax imposed on the value of property passed to others because of your death. (In other words, when you die and your property is transferred in name to your heirs or designees, the change of ownership is a taxable event.) If your estate is large enough, the tax applies to the *taxable* estate: your *gross estate less allowable deductions.*

The gross estate generally includes the value of *all* property—usually the fair market value on the date of death, although an executor may elect an alternative valuation date, such as six months after the date of death— as well as the following (these can vary, so check with a CPA or attorney to determine if these apply to your estate):

- Life insurance proceeds payable to the estate or, if you owned the policy, to your heirs
- The value of certain annuities payable to the estate, or your heirs
- The value of certain property transferred within three years of your death
- Trusts or other interests established by you, or others in which you have certain powers

Allowable *deductions* generally include the following:

- Funeral expenses paid out of your estate
- Debts you owed at the time of death
- The marital deduction (usually the value of all property that passes from your estate to your spouse)

The tax is calculated on your taxable estate above the applicable *exclusion amount*. In other words, if the dollar value of your taxable estate

TAXABLE ESTATE EXCLUSION AMOUNTS

Year	Exclusion Amount	Tax Rate
2005	$1,500,000	47%
2006	$2,000,000	46%
2007	$2,000,000	45%
2008	$2,000,000	45%
2009	$3,500,000	45%
2010	0	No tax this year*
2011	$1,000,000	55%

2.6 *The federal estate tax is being temporarily phased out by the Economic Growth and Tax Relief Reconciliation Act of 2001, and will, therefore, be "zero" in 2010. However, unless the tax code is changed in the near future, in 2011 the tax rate returns to its original level of 55 percent.

TAXABLE ESTATE EXAMPLE

Eleanor Smith dies a widower on August 12, 2005, and her property is valued as follows:

$1,500,000	Farm
800,000	Personal property
300,000	Life insurance
$2,600,000	**Total value of gross estate**

She only has one heir, Allison Smith, her daughter. To determine the taxable estate, we need to subtract the allowable deductions.

$2,600,000	Total value of gross estate
- 10,000	Funeral expenses and costs of settling the estate
- 300,000	Debts owed by Eleanor (mortgage, credit cards, etc.)
0	Marital deduction (none—because her spouse predeceased her)
$2,290,000	**Total value of taxable estate**

Because the taxable estate is above the exclusion amount of $1,500,000 (see fig. 2.6), Allison will have to pay federal estate tax. Like the income tax, the federal estate tax is a *progressive* tax—rates vary at different levels of estate value. The highest marginal tax rate in 2005 is 47 percent, so Allison owes approximately $361,300.

is *less than* the exclusion amount, you don't owe any estate tax. I've included a chart showing the exclusion amount and highest marginal estate tax rate applicable by year (fig. 2.6).

Families with farms, or other highly appreciated property, can be caught unaware by the federal estate tax. If you think your estate will be sizeable, consult an experienced attorney or CPA to help you minimize the amount of taxes that will be owed, and plan for a method of payment. The basic rule is that the estate tax return must be filed and any tax due must be paid within nine months after the decedent's death. Extensions may be granted upon request to the IRS.

IRS Publication 950, *Introduction to Estate and Gift Taxes*, provides more insight into the calculation of your taxable estate.

TRUSTS

A *trust* is property owned or managed by a person (the *trustee*) for the benefit of another (the *beneficiary*). Trusts can be either *inter vivos* (created during the grantor's lifetime to benefit the grantor himself, or someone else) or *testamentary* (created through a will).

The property placed (or transferred) into a trust is called the *principal* or *corpus*. This can be any type of property, although real estate and other investments, such as stocks and bonds, are the most common. The *trust agreement* dictates how the property will be managed, the powers of the trustee, and when the trust will end and its assets distributed to the beneficiaries. Some trusts are designed to only last a short time, until a minor reaches the age of 30, for example, and others are designed to last longer, even someone's entire lifetime. State law determines how long a trust can be in existence—some states not allowing perpetual (never-ending) trusts, is one such rule.

The trustee is responsible for managing the property according to terms in the trust agreement, and if he fails to act prudently, he can be held accountable for his actions or any loss of value to the property in the trust. The trustee does not have to be an individual; corporate entities, such as banks or trust companies, can be "professional" trustees.

Reasons for creating a trust include:

- Holding family wealth as it passes from one generation to the next

- Investment and property management

- Keeping trust assets free from marital claims by present or future spouses of trust beneficiaries (i.e., circumventing sons- and daughters-in-law)

- Protecting the grantor's family or dependents against demands from other family members

- Managing a business interest after death until it can be sold or taken over by intended heirs

- Protecting trust beneficiaries against themselves when they are too young or mentally and physically incapable of managing property

- Protecting beneficiaries from creditors (a *spendthrift clause* can prevent a beneficiary from assigning or encumbering trust assets, i.e. a creditor cannot claim those trust assets)

You can make your horse a beneficiary of a trust. In the event there is no one to bequeath your horse to, this may be a good alternative to a will provision. According to Mr. Zwerdling, one of the easiest ways to do this is to create a testamentary trust, fund it with life insurance, and make your estate the beneficiary. The trustee can arrange for your horse to be cared for until the horse's death, at which time any remaining funds are distributed according to your wishes.

There are costs associated with creating and maintaining a trust. Trustees, like executors, receive compensation for their work (posting bonds, managing investments, and making filings, among other required duties). The fees charged by professional trustees vary; however, they are usually a minimum based on the value of the property in trust: for example, a trust with $4,000,000 principal invested in mutual funds might have an annual fee of .34 percent or $13,600; and the same size trust with an individually managed portfolio of stocks and bonds may cost .70 percent or $28,000 each year.

A local attorney qualified in these matters can explain estate laws and the benefits, drawbacks, and costs of the different types of trusts allowed in your state.

ALTERNATIVE MEASURES

While discussing unpleasant topics, like death and taxes, here is another item for your consideration: suppose you own an older, arthritic horse with special needs and suddenly you become chronically ill or are otherwise unable to take care for him. In such a scenario, humane euthanasia is a viable alternative to selling your horse, giving him away, or having family members dispose of him at an auction to an unknown, possibly unpleasant fate.

Part IV
MARITAL AND PERSONAL AGREEMENTS

Pre- and Post-Nuptial Agreements

The very idea of asking your fiancé or spouse to sign a pre- or post-nuptial agreement concerning disposition of personal and real property in the event of divorce is distasteful—you may feel you are dooming your relationship before it even begins. It is a personal choice to be considered carefully.

As a general rule, anything you purchased *before* marriage is considered pre-marital property and therefore "yours." Anything you purchase *afterward* becomes part of the marital property and must be distributed in a divorce. With a legal agreement, spousal support and property distribution (including who gets the horses) is spelled out, often helping ease some of the animosity separation can breed.

Marital agreements prepared by an attorney cost between $500 and $1,000.

Personal Agreements

It is often the case that you "discover" horses, or delve into a business that involves horses, with a partner or friend. Whether a couple or just friends, it is imperative to keep good records, and draw up an agreement that spells out your respective contributions to the ownership or lease of a horse (if that be the case), or the hobby or business that you are involved in together. The agreement should contain provisions for the termination and subsequent disposition of related funds and property, including any animals involved. Jeffrey Zwerdling knows of heated and bitter battles fought over dogs. "It happens all the time," he says. "A couple gets a house or an apartment together, and then they buy a dog...They split up, and can't agree on who should get the dog."

A personal agreement drafted by an attorney costs between $200 and $500.

Hard Decisions

In the event a separation seems inevitable, speak privately with an attorney beforehand—he'll provide "damage control." In addition, I suggest speaking with a counselor, such as a licensed clinical social worker, who can help you view your situation from a variety of angles. Financial decisions made in the heat of the moment are based on emotion and are not beneficial in the long term. Professional help can enable you to make informed decisions, instead.

The intent of chapter 2 has been to provide a broad overview of personal financial management, and the information provided is not a substitute for legal, investment, or accounting advice that only a professional, familiar with your particular circumstances, can provide you.

CHAPTER THREE

Their Barn or Yours?

I t is pouring rain and there's an arctic chill in the air. The commute home from work was awful—it seems people always forget how to drive in bad weather. You had planned to go to the barn to ride, but as you watch the water run down the window panes, a hot cup of tea and a snuggle on the couch with the magazine you have been meaning to read is far more appealing. You feel a twinge of guilt, but it quickly passes as you drift into a nap before dinner. Aahhh…the luxury of boarding your horse.

If you have horses on your property, or lease a barn or stable and manage it yourself, this scenario plays out a little differently. While you can still have your cup of tea, you can forget the couch! Instead, you will dutifully pull on your boots, gloves, hat, and ski pants (my personal favorite), brave the elements, and complete the barn chores. Taking care of your own horses requires dedication, but for some, there is no better reward than walking out the door of the house and into the barn where beautiful, bright-eyed horses eagerly await.

At the beginning of this book, I mentioned that one of the decisions you must make as a horse owner is whether to board your horse out or keep him at home. As you can see, each has its benefits. Most of the chapters that follow detail the expense of owning or acquiring a horse property, but in this chapter, I illustrate the pros, cons, and costs of each, enabling you to not only make an informed decision between the two, but also to examine eligible boarding facilities with a discerning eye.

Boarding

Commitment

Horses are labor intensive and involve a huge time commitment: at least twice a day, every day, they need to be fed, watered, and otherwise tended. If you have a work commute, a job that requires frequent overnight travel, or a career that demands relentless overtime and Saturdays at the office, then you and your horse may be happier at a boarding facility. It is especially helpful to have someone available to hold your horse for the farrier and meet the veterinarian for routine shots or emergency care—appointments that usually happen during "normal working hours."

"Often, people think that having a horse in the backyard would be nice and just go out and purchase a horse," says Junior Johnson, a hunt seat equitation instructor and manager of Foxwood Farm near Crozier, Virginia. "…they have no idea what to do with it or how to take care of it… People don't realize how much work having a horse is and how much time it takes. It is like having a job (where) you're on-call for twenty-four hours a day."

Mr. Johnson says that some of his clients throughout the years simply moved to the country and bought a horse—without a clue how to care for or handle a horse properly. These clients soon realized they were in over their heads. In such cases, even when the horse owner has already purchased a "horse property," the better option for all involved is to find a nearby boarding facility and learn the ropes before bringing the horse home.

Environment

One of the positives of choosing to board is the acquisition "by association" of what is often a much nicer facility than you could afford to own. As you and your horse will be spending a lot of time in this environment, it is important that you both feel safe and comfortable. There are several specific areas that should be considered when comparing boarding stables. I discuss them in detail in *Choosing a Boarding Facility*.

Diet

Often, new horse owners know little about how to determine what a horse should be fed. A good boarding stable will provide consistent nutrition by feeding the best quality hay and grain available. Management will choose the types and amounts suitable for your horse with respect to age, condition, exercise level, and your own goals as the owner and rider (for example, preparing for an upper level event or starting your seven-year-old daughter in the local short-stirrup division). Obviously, having knowledgeable professionals to recommend or make dietary adjustments so your horse can attain peak performance can be a great asset.

Social Aspects

There are many social benefits to boarding your horse. The nature of a boarding stable—bringing people with the same interest together in a limited space—lends itself to becoming a meeting place. Many people go to their boarding barn to enjoy themselves, chat with their friends, and relax—as well as spend time with their horses and ride. For those who are uncomfortable with horse management, this atmosphere provides a constant source of help and opinions. In this way, boarding provides a "support group," especially if management is there to lend a hand.

Choosing a Boarding Facility

If you've read this far and determined that the best choice for you and your horse is a boarding facility, then the search for an appropriate barn can begin. At first, I urge you not to limit your search by only considering barns with boarding fees in a certain price range. Comparing monthly costs at different stables becomes easier when you know what is included in each, what services will incur extra charges, and the types of facilities available in your area. Don't judge a horse facility by the board fee alone. Quality costs, but quality can save you thousands of dollars in injury and illness prevented.

Stalls and Stables

Look critically at the stalls in a prospective boarding barn. Is the size of the stall suitable for your horse? For example, you need at least 10 feet by 10 feet for a pony and 12 feet by 12 feet for a horse. Is the ceiling high enough? Will your horse be able to raise his head (or even rear) without hitting the ceiling? At least 11 feet of clearance is preferable. Do the stalls have solid partitions? Are there protruding objects such as nail heads sticking out of boards? What is the flooring in the stalls—wood, cement, clay, or rubber mats? How is drainage handled? What is the ventilation like? Does each stall have a window, or is there another system of maintaining airflow? Are you comfortable with the layout of the stable? Is the main aisle an appropriate width and clear of debris? How many sets of cross-ties are there and where are they situated? Is there a wash stall? Hot water? Obviously, this list can include other necessities or amenities you deem important in your horse's home.

Pasture and Turnout

Horses are naturally roaming, grazing animals, and it is necessary for both their physical and psychological health that they have several hours (at the very least) of turnout each day. It is, therefore, important to consider a boarding facility's pasture and paddock space. How big are the turnout areas? Is there room for boarders to be turned out together? Are mares and geldings separated? Are stallions in separate enclosures and contained appropriately? Too many horses in a confined area can potentially create dangerous situations. Ask management about turnout arrangements, how they introduce new horses into a herd, and if they take into account the state of the fields and weather.

Consider the condition of the paddocks and pastures. Does the pasture contain a good stand of grass, or is it overgrazed or full of weeds? Are all turnout spaces free of dangerous debris? Does manure appear to be removed or dragged with a harrow regularly?

Are enclosures fenced with materials considered safe for horses, such as wire-mesh, electric-tape, or four-board fencing? Barbed wire and high-tensile wire can cause serious injury if a horse becomes entangled, and should not be anywhere on the property. Is all fencing in good repair? If management conscientiously maintains fencing, it usually indicates they take the same care with the rest of the boarding facility.

Riding Facilities

Does the barn have a riding ring? Is an indoor ring available? Does it have quality footing that won't be slippery when wet or rock hard when dry? Is the footing cleaned and raked regularly? Is the ring large enough to accommodate your riding discipline or multiple riders? What kind of equipment is available (i.e., standards and rails, dressage letters, cones, barrels, etc.)? Are there trails nearby?

Management

I think management is the most important area of consideration when comparing boarding facilities. Personally, I would choose an adequate facility with quality management over a great facility with inconsistent management: a horse turned out in a field with a full water trough is far better off than a horse standing in a beautiful stall for hours without water or hay.

Take another look around the prospective barn. Do the stalls look as if they have been cleaned recently, or do you smell urine and ammonia when you walk in the door? Are there a lot of flies? Do the horses look well fed and happy? Does every horse have a full, clean bucket of water? Is the overall appearance of the stable neat and orderly?

Chat with people who board their horses at the facility, and listen to the conversations they are having with each other. Do they seem content? Ask how often management turns over (you won't get consistent care at a boarding facility without consistent staff).

Finally, talk to the barn manager and staff. Ask what management expects of boarders. Find out what is included in the board and what services are provided for an extra fee. Discuss worming schedules, routine veterinary care and vaccinations, and ask what precautions are taken to keep infectious disease, such as strangles, from becoming a problem. Go over the barn rules and hours of operation. They should make sense and be agreeable to you. As I mentioned before, you and your horse need to feel safe and comfortable in this "home away from home," as you'll be spending a lot of time—and money—there.

As Thomas J. Newton, DVM, of Crozier, Virginia, says, one of boarding's biggest pros is that you "get to enjoy horses on your terms without having them run your life." In other words, you can have that cup of tea and stay on the couch. But, while I enjoyed spending time at the barn when I boarded my horses, it always seemed that by the time I drove there, rode, groomed, piddled around the place, and drove home, it was ten o'clock at night—and I still had to eat dinner! For me, just being in the barn and taking care of the horse is as rewarding as riding; sometimes more so, because in the end, you spend more time care-taking than riding. Feeling this way about your horse and his needs is the first step in "bringing him home" to your own property.

HORSES AT HOME

Commitment

If you have a routine work schedule and your employer's environment allows you some flexibility, having horses at home may be a viable option. Meeting the farrier and veterinarian, and receiving deliveries of hay, grain, and bedding require you to be at home during normal working hours (though you can schedule your appointments early in the morning or late in the day to lessen time spent away from your job).

In addition to your "workstyle," your lifestyle must be able to accommodate the labor and time spent caring for your horse. So, if you have school age children who participate in a variety of activities and sports and you already have a hard time fitting them all in, you should seriously consider the impact one *more* time commitment—your horse—will have on your family's well-being. Or, if you enjoy weekend getaways and extended vacations, realize that a knowledgeable "horse-sitter" will have to be acquired (and paid for) whenever you choose to leave home.

Environment

One of the benefits of taking care of your own horses is that you can control their environment. While your barn might not be as glamorous as the boarding stable down the road, you can be sure it is the cleanest, safest space for your horse to inhabit. For example, if you happen to have one of those horses that is a magnet for accidents and injuries, and has "bite me" written on his rump, you can determine when and for how long he is turned out, and whether or not your old pony mare accompanies him. You can minimize the scope and frequency of injuries by manipulating his physical environment, and in the end, you can go to the show the following weekend without new mystery swellings or plugs of hair missing.

Stable Management

Dr. Newton points out that some people like to control every aspect of their horse's care, in a sense "micromanage" the horse. For example, if you want your horse's blanket changed each time the temperature alters a few degrees, you may be better off keeping your horse at your own barn. When your horse is in your own barn, you are the one scraping the stall floor clean and scattering lime, scrubbing his water and feed buckets daily, and keeping sharp edges and other potential hazards to a minimum. There is something to be said for the "peace of mind" achieved when you are the individual responsible for these things.

Diet

When your horse is at home, you can personally control his diet with a specific purpose and lifestyle in mind. Of course, this is a learned process. First-time horse owners will need to do their homework, but there are numerous books on equine nutrition, cooperatives and feed stores often offer management seminars, and your veterinarian can give you insight, as well. It is important to learn what types of hay are available locally and which of the various commercial grain products are readily sold in your area.

The effects grain-type or feed-brand can have on your horse can be truly amazing. For example, you may have an older, relatively inactive horse you like to trail ride on the weekends. An energy-bar diet of 16-percent-protein sweet feed and alfalfa hay would likely transform your sweet little pleasure horse into an aspiring racehorse. On the other hand, the young reining prospect you work five nights a week might need that high-protein diet to keep his energy level high and condition prime. In either case, the benefits of "feeding what you ride" are evident.

Understanding "Normal"

Caring for your horse every day allows you to get to know him. You see how much water he drinks, how fast he eats, and his habits and quirks. By learning the "normal and routine," you can identify the "out-of-the-ordinary," realize he isn't "acting himself," and immediately investigate. Early intervention and a prompt call to the vet when your horse is ill can make recovery easier.

Communication

It is possible to have the type of relationship with a horse that many people have with their favorite dog. I have had dogs all my life—about ten in all—and of those, three have been outstanding. These were the dogs that always tried to please. They could judge how I felt just by looking at me and knew just the right thing to do to get my attention so I'd forget my troubles. They have enriched my life and made me laugh. Horses are capable of the same attachment and desire to please you. It evolves from a combination of intelligence, personality, life experience, and the way they are treated on a daily basis. Having your horse at home where you can spend the maximum amount of time with him can promote this evolution. Your relationship as friends and partners can potentially reach a new level.

BEFORE YOU BRING YOUR HORSE HOME, ASK YOURSELF:

- *Are you willing to clean stalls several times a day?*
  I enjoy cleaning stalls; it is one of the few things I do in life that shows immediate results, and it's relaxing. There is an art to maximizing cleanliness and minimizing wasted bedding. But, to some it remains a laborious, time-consuming chore involving urine and manure.

- *Can you learn to properly inspect your hay?*
  Even if you have scrumptious-looking bales in your loft purchased from your recommended local farmer, hay must be inspected. Each bale should be opened and searched for weeds, mold, and dust, as well as items that may have inadvertently ended up in the bale (such as cans, bottles, snakes, squirrels, or rope). Sometimes, hay is not harvested under perfect conditions and ends up coarse or dusty.

- *Can you learn to identify poisonous plants, shrubs, and trees?*
  You will need to know which vegetation around the house and barn is poisonous to your horse. Once, when some friends of mine were visiting, their small children were picking flowers near the edge of the woods and I just happened to notice as they were about to feed my horses a lovely collection of morning glory—a hallucinogen. There are many common weeds and leaves that, if ingested by a horse, can cause a variety of problems. It is important to familiarize yourself with the native species in your area and which ones might be toxic so you can be sure your pasture areas are safe.

DIRECT COST COMPARISON

When choosing between boarding out and keeping your horse at home, one of the most important questions to ask yourself is, *"Which choice is more affordable?"* Unfortunately, this is not an easy question to answer. Everyone's situation is unique, but I've provided several scenarios to help you quantify the possible differences in costs.

Scenario One

You own a house in a subdivision with a $250,000 balance remaining on the mortgage. You also own one horse and are currently paying $450 per

- ***Can you lift 50 pounds easily?***
  Hay bales weigh 50 to 60 pounds each; grain bags and large salt blocks weigh 50 pounds; and a full, 5-gallon bucket of water weighs about 40 pounds. Though you can arrange to have your hay and grain delivered and unloaded for you, it is a very good idea to be physically capable of moving these items yourself on a daily basis.

- ***Are you willing to learn how to take your horse's temperature and bandage a wound in the event of an injury?***
  Horses are very good at getting coughs, scrapes, and bumps, so if you are going to keep your horse at home, you need to have a basic knowledge of equine triage.

- ***Are you planning on purchasing additional horses or companion animals?***
  It is important to note that horses are herd animals and generally don't fare well when isolated from their own kind. If you only own one horse and want to keep him at home, you will need to consider acquiring a retired or disabled companion horse or a boarder, which of course means additional work!

- ***How does your spouse or partner feel about having horses at home?***
  Will your significant other be making his or her own "lifestyle sacrifice" to support your love of horses? Remember the "commitment" aspect when keeping horses on your own property—you might be ready to give up your weekend getaways, but is your partner? It is important to consider the effect your horse activities will have on the other members of your household.

month in board, plus $75 per month in fees for additional services, such as blanketing and holding your horse for the farrier.

You've found a 10-acre "dream farm" with a nice house, barn, and fenced pastures that requires you to borrow $325,000. Attribute the $75,000 difference between the mortgages to the cost of acquiring "horse property," so roughly 23 percent of the total amount borrowed will go into calculating your horse-keeping expense (fig. 4.1).

Scenario One
CALCULATING "HORSE-KEEPING" MORTGAGE STEP 1

$325,000   Proposed mortgage
- *$250,000*   Existing mortgage
$75,000   Extra mortgage cost associated with moving to a farm

$75,000 ÷ $325,000 = **.23 (23 percent)**

23 percent of the new mortgage can be attributed to horse-keeping expenses. (On average, 18 to 25 percent of the total value of an established horse property—stable, ring, and fenced pastures—can be attributed to "horse-keeping" expenses.)

4.1

A 30-year mortgage for $325,000 with a fixed interest rate of 7 percent will require an approximate payment of $2,162 per month (not including insurance and real estate taxes). Therefore, $497 (23 percent) of your monthly payment can be listed on your horse's expense worksheet (fig. 4.2).

Scenario One
CALCULATING "HORSE-KEEPING" MORTGAGE STEP 2

$2162   Proposed monthly mortgage payment
x .23   Percent of new mortgage attributed to horse-keeping expenses
$497   Amount of monthly mortgage payment associated with horse-keeping

4.2

AVERAGE MONTHLY EXPENDITURES FOR ONE HORSE

- *Pasture maintenance* for 8 acres, including costs for fertilizer, lime, seed, and weed spray (applied by the local agricultural store) costs $1,650 per year or **$137.50** per month

- Barn *maintenance* (replacing broken fence boards and blown light bulbs, for example) and barn *utilities* (water and electicity) costs $720 per year or **$60** per month.

- 100 bales of *hay* per year at $4.50 per bale costs $450 per year or **$38** per month

- 6 pounds of *grain* (sweet feed only) per day at $9 per bag (not including sales tax) costs $408 per year or **$34** per month

- *Bedding* (pine shavings delivered in bulk) at $200 per 20 cubic yards costs $480 per year or **$40** per month

- *Salt and minerals* costs $72 per year or **$6** per month

4.3 Veterinary care, farriery, worming, supplements, and grooming supplies (such as fly spray) do not figure into this calculation as these costs are out of your pocket both at a boarding facility and at home.

Scenario One
MONTHLY COST WORKSHEET FOR ONE HORSE

Fixed costs*

Horse property	$497
Pasture maintenance	138
Maintenance and utilities	60
Total fixed costs	**$695**

Variable costs*

Hay	$ 38
Grain	34
Bedding	40
Salt and minerals	6
Total variable costs	**$118**

Cost per month	**$813** to keep a horse on your own property

4.4 *Under a *direct-costing* system for manufacturing, costs are classified as either *fixed*—those that remain constant whether one item is produced or a hundred items are produced—or *variable*—those that fluctuate in direct proportion to changes in the number of items produced. For the purposes of this book, our "item" or "unit of production" is one horse.

If you recall, when you were living in the subdivision, your boarding fee and extra horse costs came to a total of $525 per month. Our cost worksheet tells us that if you purchase the dream farm, the approximate total cost of keeping your horse at home will be $813 per month (figs. 4.3 & 4.4). So, staying in your current house and continuing to board is the more economical route. *However*, when calculating affordability in the long run, you should also take into account possible tax deductibility of interest paid per month, as well as potential property appreciation.

The Effect of Tax-Deductible Interest

In Scenario One, the total interest paid on the new mortgage during the first year is $22,645. Remember, you are attributing 23 percent of the new mortgage to horse-keeping expenses, therefore, 23 percent of the interest paid during the first year can be figured into your horse cost worksheet. Assuming you are in a 25 percent marginal tax bracket, the amount of your monthly mortgage payment attributable to horse-keeping expense is now around $389 per month instead of $497 per month (fig. 4.5).

Investment Considerations

When you purchase a piece of property, it is helpful to remember it will usually *appreciate in value*. Therefore, if you sell it somewhere down the line, you will recoup some of your costs.

For example, let's say the total price of your dream farm is $370,000 (as discussed previously, you borrow $325,000 in order to make the purchase). Maybe twelve years from now you will resell the property for $444,000—a 20 percent increase in overall value. If you spread the $74,000 worth of appreciated value over the period of your ownership, your real estate "investment" earns $513 per month. As with the other equations, 23 percent of the "earnings"—$118—can be attributed to keeping horses on your own property (fig. 4.6).

If you combine the percent of investment return related to keeping horses at home with the tax benefits of deductible interest, your fixed cost for your "horse property" (as listed in your cost worksheet) over a period of time is actually around $271 per month (figs. 4.7 & 4.8).

Now, you were boarding your horse for $525 per month, and it would cost approximately $587 per month to keep your horse at home. Remaining in your current house and continuing to board still seems the more economical route. If you own more than one horse, however, in the

---

CALCULATING TAX-DEDUCTIBLE INTEREST EFFECT

$25,944	Total first year mortgage payments ($2,162 x 12 months = $25,944)
22,645	Total interest paid in the first year
$5,208	23 percent of total interest paid in the first year ($22,645 x .23 = $5,208) (The amount of interest attributable to horse-keeping expenses)

* * *

1,302	Yearly savings with interest deductibility ($5,208 x .25 = $1,302)
$108	Monthly savings ($1,302 ÷ 12 months = $108)

* * *

497	Monthly mortgage payment attributed to horse-keeping *before* interest deductibility
- 108	Monthly savings after figuring interest deductibility
$ 389	Monthly mortgage payment attributed to horse-keeping *after* interest deductibility

4.5   Figures are rounded to the nearest whole number

CALCULATING INVESTMENT EARNINGS

$74,000	Amount gained in resale of farm ($444,000 - $370,000 = $74,000)
$513	Amount farm "earns" per month over period of your ownership ($74,000 ÷ 144* = $513.00)
$118	Amount keeping horse on own property "earns" per month over period of your ownership ($513 x .23 = $118)

* (12 years x 12 months = 144 months)

4.6

CALCULATING COST OF HORSE PROPERTY OVER PERIOD OF TIME

$389 Amount of mortgage attributed to horse-keeping after interest deductibility

- *$118* Amount keeping horses on own property "earns" in investment return

$271 Amount horse property costs per month over period of time
($389 - $118 = $271)

4.7

Scenario One
MONTHLY COST WORKSHEET FOR ONE HORSE
(after figuring interest deductibility and investment return)

Fixed costs

Horse property	$271
Pasture maintenance	138
Maintenance and utilities	60
Total fixed costs	**$469**

Variable costs

Hay	$ 38
Grain	34
Bedding	40
Salt and minerals	6
Total variable costs	**$118**
Cost per month	**$587** to keep a horse on your own property

4.8

---

long run, buying the dream farm and keeping them at home would be the financially beneficial choice. Your *fixed costs* on your worksheet won't change if you add another horse to the picture; only your *variable costs* will increase (fig. 4.9).

Boarding two horses at the rates mentioned earlier costs $1,050 per month, while keeping those horses on your new dream farm costs only

---

Scenario One
MONTHLY COST WORKSHEET FOR TWO HORSES

Fixed costs

Horse property	$271
Pasture maintenance	138
Maintenance and utilities	60
Total fixed costs	**$469**

Variable costs

Hay	$ 76
Grain	68
Bedding	80
Salt and minerals	12
Total variable costs	**$236**
Cost per month	**$705** to keep two horses on your own property

4.9

$705 per month. If you have three horses, it costs $1,575 to board all of them and $823 to keep them on your own property. Clearly, there are economies of scale: the more horses you own and keep on your own property, the more the "unit cost" of each horse decreases. If you already own more than one horse, or if you are contemplating purchasing more horses, owning horse property is probably more economically feasible than boarding all your animals.

Scenario Two

You are currently paying $375 per month for board, plus $50 per month for extra services such as blanketing and holding your horse for the farrier. You have found a piece of land that would be perfect for the horse estate you've always imagined. In Scenario One, your dream farm's house, barn, and ring were already completed, but this time, you will have to figure in the costs of clearing, grading, building a house and barn, establishing a ring and pasture, and fencing. The costs associated with the barn, pasture, ring, and fencing will be listed on your horse expense worksheet (see figs. 4.10 & 4.13).

Scenario Two
APPROXIMATE COSTS

Price of 6 acres at $2,000 per acre	$12,000
Clearing and grading 6 acres of pasture	10,000
Seeding, fertilizing, liming 6 acres of pasture	1,500
Fencing 6 acres, including materials & labor	11,000
Building a four-stall barn with tack room	35,000
Grading a ring	2,000
Ring footing (stone dust and sand)	6,000
Total costs for horse-related items	**$77,500**

4.10 Actual costs will vary depending on your location and current lumber and material prices. This example assumes you will be hiring a general contractor for all of the work.

Scenario Two
CALCULATING "HORSE-KEEPING" MORTGAGE STEP 1

$222,500	Cost of non-horse-related acreage and improvements
+ 77,500	Total costs for horse-related acreage and improvements
$300,000	Total cost of property and establishing dream farm ($222,500 + $77,500 = $300,000)
26 percent	Percent of total cost attributed to keeping your horse at home ($77,500 ÷ $300,000 = .26)

4.11

Scenario Two
CALCULATING "HORSE-KEEPING" MORTGAGE STEP 2

$1,996	Proposed monthly mortgage payment
x .26	Percent of new mortgage attributed to horse-keeping expenses
$519	Amount of monthly mortgage payment associated with horse-keeping

4.12

Scenario Two
MONTHLY COST WORKSHEET FOR ONE HORSE

Fixed costs

Horse property	$519
*Pasture maintenance (6 acres)	100
Maintenance and utilities	60
Total fixed costs	**$679**

Variable costs

Hay	$ 38
Grain	34
Bedding	40
Salt and minerals	6
Total variable costs	**$118**
Cost per month	**$797** to keep a horse on your own property

4.13   * The cost of pasture maintenance in Scenerio Two reflects ownership of two fewer acres than Scenario One.

In this example, the remaining acreage and cost of building your home is $222,500. If we add this to the cost of horse-related items, the total cost of purchasing the new property and establishing your farm is $300,000. Therefore, roughly 26 percent of the total cost could be attributed to keeping your horse at home (fig. 4.11).

If you financed the full $300,000 using a 30-year, fixed rate mortgage at 7 percent interest per year, your mortgage payment would be approximately $1,996 per month (not including real estate taxes or insurance). Of that monthly payment, 26 percent—$519—could be considered attributable to acquiring a horse property (fig. 4.12).

If you compare your total boarding costs of $425 per month to almost $800 per month to keep your horse at home, continuing to board is the more economical route. However, this example does not illustrate the benefits of mortgage interest deductibility and the ultimate return on your investment if you sell the property at some point in the future, which will increase the difference when factored in (see pp. 71–3).

Again, the more horses you own, the more financially sound the decision to purchase rural real estate and care for them yourself becomes (for example, three horses in Scenario Two would cost $1,275 per month to board and only $1,033 to keep at home). Of course, just because it would be "cheaper" in the long run to have four or five horses on your own property, does not mean that you can afford four or five horses—remember the out-of-pocket expenses and time commitment more animals will entail, neither of which are included on our horse-cost worksheets.

If you have determined that the benefits of keeping your horse at home outweigh the benefits of boarding, and you can afford the move to your own farm, then you can begin to search for a horse property.

CHAPTER FOUR

Purchasing Horse Property

Fulfilling your dream of owning a farm property can be a wonderful lifestyle change. If you own a couple of horses, or plan to buy more, it can be the economically sound choice to make, as illustrated in the last chapter. However, finding and purchasing a property—dealing with real estate agents, lenders, and attorneys—can be difficult and stressful, and it's helpful to know how to avoid "surprises," especially expensive ones! This chapter is not intended to provide definitive legal advice or be a comprehensive guide to all considerations and pitfalls, but more of an outline of what to expect. I always suggest enlisting the help of first, a real estate agent, and later, an attorney, to guide you through the process.

THE SEARCH

When you are serious about buying a horse property, there are several ways to find one, including "word-of-mouth" (some sellers depend on this method in order to avoid the fees associated with advertising), classified ads, and real estate agencies. Agencies maintain listings of available properties, and these are often available online or in a print catalog.

Real Estate Agents

Whether you are looking for an existing farm ready for horses, a house with enough land to develop into a horse property, or raw land where you can build your own home, enlist the assistance of a local licensed real estate agent to help you search in the area and act as a liaison between you and a seller.

Real estate agents are licensed by a state either as *brokers* or *agents*. *Brokers* are licensed to run a real estate business: they've completed required courses and apprenticeships, passed exams, and survived personal finance and credit audits. *Agents* work for brokers: while they've passed required exams and are licensed, they can only sell property under a broker's authority. *Realtors*® are brokers and agents who have taken an oath to abide by the National Association of Realtors (NAR) code of ethics; they sponsor the Multiple Listing Service (MLS), which provides a comprehensive listing of all properties for sale, under contract, or sold. (Note: properties for sale by owner are usually not listed here.)

Typically, there are *seller's agents* and *buyer's agents*, and both work on commission or for a fee. A seller's agent works solely for the seller of a property and the percentage of the selling price that will be paid to his agency, so as a buyer, it is in your best interests not to trust him completely. A buyer's agent, on the other hand, represents your best interests. If a buyer's agent shows you a property listed for sale by his company, then he works for a *dual agency*—in cases like this, beware: a conflict of interest can arise when it comes to finalizing a purchase price.

When choosing an agent, begin by asking around. Agents' reputations tend to precede them, and certain agencies may be recommended as more trustworthy than others. Arrange a meeting with a potential agent before hiring him, and ask questions about the usual price range of the properties he handles and his preferred geographical area of expertise. In some areas of the country, you can find agents who specialize in horse properties, and their knowledge and experience can prove extremely useful during your search, especially if you are a first-time buyer. Most, however, are not going to be horsemen, so familiarize yourself with some of the special considerations that make property suitable for horses (see p. 135 for some examples).

Provide your agent a rough description of the type of property you are interested in, as well as the price range you can afford (if you aren't certain how much you can spend, your agent can help you determine a figure, as well as guide you through the process of loan pre-qualification). You will be given a specification sheet for each listed property that fits your description, including details such as an acreage survey, descriptions of buildings on the parcel, and property cost specifics. Should any of these interest you, he can assist with many of the issues I discuss on the following pages—including clarification of zoning and land restrictions and acquiring thorough building inspections, to name a few—which will save you a great deal of leg work.

What to Look For

There are many things to consider when moving to a rural area that may increase costs of living. You must also remember that just because a property is "rural," it doesn't necessarily mean it is appropriate for horse-keeping. Bear these two important aspects in mind as you evaluate a parcel's land, structures, and overall appeal.

Road Frontage and Accessibility

Does the prospective property have state- or town-maintained road frontage? Living on a private road without the usual traffic nuisances may initially seem to be an attractive proposition, but be aware that you can incur large, unexpected bills. For instance, if the majority of neighboring landowners decide to re-gravel the road, you will have to contribute your share—and similar costs may occur suddenly if the road is washed out. You will also have to budget for additional large *expected* bills, like plowing and sanding in northern climates. A long private road costs quite a bit to maintain throughout the winter months, even when the burden is shared by neighbors.

When it comes time to finance your purchase (see p. 94) some institutional lenders (banks or mortgage companies, for example) will be reluctant to approve a loan on property that doesn't have public road frontage. If your heart is set on land with a private road, lenders will usually require a copy of the *road maintenance agreement* (the legal document recorded at the local courthouse, binding all owners who share use of the road to certain terms). It will also give you an idea of yearly maintenance costs.

Consider the *isolation level* of the property. How far away is the nearest grocery store, gas station, and school? How far is the property from emergency services, such as a fire department and rescue squad? If you are a great distance from these and other service-providers, additional personal preparation—and related expense—must be considered.

How many other houses and/or farms are serviced by the same power and telephone lines? The more remote you are, the lower you will be on the priority list for restoration services, and in addition, you will need to consider the possible cost of purchasing an alternative power source, such as a generator (see sidebar).

Think about your goals as an equestrian. Do you plan to compete frequently? If so, consider the distance to other riding facilities. Easy access to a main thoroughfare might be desirable. Twisting, narrow, and dirt roads and driveways can make hauling horses more difficult—and discourage truckers from delivering hay or farm machinery.

ELECTRICITY AND WATER—FROM THE HORSE'S VIEWPOINT

Remote properties are often served by wells rather than public water sources, and well pumps are run by electricity. One horse can consume 10 to 20 gallons of water per day, and without sufficient intake, they are prone to colic. It is, therefore, extremely important on a farm that an alternative source of electricity is available to ensure the availability of fresh water during extended power failures.

Generators, depending on their size, type, and fuel needs, cost between $500 and $3,500. A small, quality gas generator with enough output to run a well pump can be purchased for under $1,000 from most vendors.

On the other hand, if looking at property on a main road, different concerns should be taken into account. The constant flow of traffic and resulting noise will affect you, your family, and your horses. Traffic is a potential hazard when a horse gets loose, and easy access to your home, barn, and pasture can also be a security threat. (The "up-side" to being on a main road is that your horse grows accustomed to noise and seeing vehicles pass by his pasture, which acclimates him to things he will potentially encounter outside the ring.)

A property may appeal to you either because it's "off the beaten path," or because it's easily accessible. While both scenarios can certainly prove ideal in the end, it is important to critically consider exactly how property location will impact your life before making a purchase.

Barn Location

A property may already have a horse barn, but is that barn well situated? If you are planning on building your facility, is there an appropriate place for it? Before you seriously consider a property, you need to take a look at the way outbuildings are arranged with respect to the land and each other. (Information on structures and property planning can be found on in chapter 5.)

Drainage is often a problem, and barns built in low, wet areas host an assortment of difficulties from large fly populations to equine health problems. A building on a steep hill, however, can cause worrisome erosion, and in wintry climates, can be dangerously slippery and difficult to negotiate for both horse and human. *Wind, sun,* and *soil type* also impact the quality of your horse facility. The local extension service can assist you in determining the best sites for the barn, pastures, and riding ring. An agent will look over a property with you prior to purchase, and his services are free. (For more about soil type and topography, see p. 111.)

Pasture Potential

How many acres of pasture does the prospective property have? What is the quality and condition of the fencing? What is the quality of the grass? If you are buying acreage with the intent of creating pasture space, consider the length of time it will take to establish and the additional cost of the hay you will need to feed in the interim. I discuss the ins-and-outs of this process in more detail on p. 112.

Riding Space

Is there a riding ring or a flat area appropriate for schooling? Grading will be an expensive addition to your budget. Do you have access to trails or quiet roads where you and your horse can safely travel? Hauling your horse miles down the road every time you want to ride is not ideal and will probably limit the time you spend on horseback.

Overall Appeal

The first farm you see might be absolutely perfect, or you may travel to half a dozen prospective properties. When a property does meet your initial criteria and is within your price range, there are specific areas that require particular attention.

THE PRE-PURCHASE EXAM

Buying a horse property is not unlike buying a horse. As I described in chapter 1, once you've found a horse you really like, it is important for

BUYING RAW LAND

Unimproved property (land without a house or other structures) requires special attention to some key elements. Below are a few of the more critical things to consider when looking at raw land with the intent of building a horse farm. (Related discussion can be found in chapter 5, p. 103.)

Timbered Property

If you intend to clear for pasture or buildings, realize that the timber (trees) has value and you can have it appraised before you place a contract on the property. If it is mature or desirable in the local lumber market, the sale of the timber could offset the cost of clearing. Speak with a representative of your state's Department of Forestry, or a professional independent forester to get a ballpark idea of what the timber is worth or to help you locate a qualified appraiser.

Ask the seller if there are outstanding, or open timber contracts on the property—he may have previously sold the timber to a logging company, and the contract may not have been recorded in the land records and so won't be disclosed in a title search (see p. 88).

Soil Composition

You may have visions of green fields full of orchard grass and clover, but the soil on a prospective property might not be well suited to such growth—or will require extraordinary amounts of lime and fertilizer. Soil composition can vary within a few miles, or even on the same parcel of land.

Obtain a copy of your county's *soil survey* prepared by the United States Natural Resource Conservation Service from your local cooperative extension service agent. Usually, the soil survey maps out an entire county, designating different soil types, and by locating your subject property on the map, you can determine its particularities.

your veterinarian to determine the animal will continue to be sound and physically suitable for your purposes. Similarly, after you have seen a great prospective property, there are various steps you need to take to ensure your potential purchase will indeed fit your needs.

Survey information can include:

- Typical crop and pasture yields, per acre
- The soil's desirability for supporting building site and sanitary facility development
- The soil's tendency to shrink and swell in periods of dry, then wet weather (which can lead to structural damage in a foundation)
- Erosion risk
- Wetness

This information helps determine the necessary type and depth of footings and foundations required when building structures (which affects building costs), and also gauges how fertile the soil is so you can estimate the price of developing new pasture, or redeveloping existing pasture.

Well and Septic

Most rural locations do not have public water and sewer. Depending on the area, water wells may be difficult to install, or good-tasting drinking water may be difficult to find, so it is a good idea to contact the local county health department, building inspections department, and several local well companies.

Land should be tested prior to purchase to make sure it will support a septic system for the house you plan to build. A "perc test" (percolation test) determines how effectively water drains through the soil and whether it will provide adequate on-site sewage treatment. Soil that is too coarse, for example, isn't capable of proper nutrient and bacteria removal, while loam and clay does a better job, but requires a large treatment area.

A perc test should be a condition of your purchase, and you may also request the seller have a well drilled (see also *Contingencies*, p. 92).

Take a Closer Look

When you decide to buy a property, all structures should be evaluated by a professional inspector (see p. 92); however, prior to purchase, it is possible for you to get a general idea of the state of a building and its accoutrements.

Have a look at the foundations of all structures. Are they concrete slabs? Wooden posts? Are there basements? Keep an eye out for signs of rotten wood, especially in floor supports, joists, and framing. Contact the county building inspector and find out what destructive pests (such as termites) are local and how to determine infestation. Ask the seller for copies of original blueprints and/or building contracts—if available—so you can see who the laborers were, what original materials were used, and what warranties were made guaranteeing against defects in construction.

House

Make a checklist of the following and do a walk-through:

- ✓ **Exterior walls** Do they appear "square"? Check condition and quality of siding.
- ✓ **Roof** Ask when it was last repaired. Look for evidence of leaks.
- ✓ **Doors** Do they open and shut snugly? Cracks around door frames can indicate bracing problems.
- ✓ **Windows** Open and close them, watching for gaps, warps, and damage.
- ✓ **Floors** Note places that slope, loose or noisy boards, and the quality of materials.
- ✓ **Interior walls and ceilings** Watch for water stains, bulges, signs of recent painting or plastering.
- ✓ **Bathrooms** Check quality and workmanship of fixtures, tiling, and caulking.
- ✓ **Kitchen** Consider the workspace and its adaptability. Will appliances be included? Check condition, age, and original cost.
- ✓ **Plumbing/water heater** Turn on multiple faucets, flush a toilet, and gauge water pressure. Watch for drips or stains that could indicate leaks. Turn on hot water, check temperature, and watch for rust. In cold climates, ask if the pipes are situated in such a way as to prevent them freezing.
- ✓ **Sewage** Determine if you have public sewage or a septic tank. Most rural properties will have a septic tank, which will necessitate obtaining a service history so you can see it has been properly cleaned and inspected.

✓ **Electricity** Availability of outlets is important in this day and age. Ask about the wiring's history.

✓ **Insulation** Ask what kind of insulation was used. Do you feel drafts as you walk around the house?

✓ **Ventilation** Is the house stuffy or musty? Are there fans and windows throughout the structure?

✓ **Heat/air conditioning** What kind of system is it and how much does it cost to run? Is it noisy?

Barn and Other Structures

The basic items on the house checklist—such as the condition of the roof, siding, wiring, and plumbing—may apply to other buildings on the property, as well. Compose a second list of requirements for your barn (stall size, condition of flooring and lighting, and location of plumbing fixtures are some examples) and note areas that might be of particular concern.

Driveways

Existing driveways should be in good condition—not rutted or washed out—and keep in mind that steep, narrow, windy drives will be a constant challenge to navigate, with or without a trailer in tow. If a bridge or culvert is in use, cast an eye over its general appearance. Both can be expensive to repair or replace.

The view should be clear in both directions where the driveway meets the main road—for you, as well as the oncoming traffic.

Surveys

It is very important that the precise boundaries of a piece of property are determined by a *survey*: a drawing that is based on the legal description in the *deed* (the document that conveys the title to a property) and shows corners and perimeter lines, *encroachments*♦, as well as the location of buildings, septic systems, and wells. (*Some* surveys will note *easements*—see discussion on the next page—as well.) Surveys are made by a team of licensed surveyors or registered civil engineers and tend to be expensive. Rates vary across the country, but can run anywhere from $75 to $100 per hour, per two-man crew. The total cost will depend on

> ═ SO YOU KNOW... ═
>
> ♦ *Encroachments* are fences or other structures that extend into the property of another owner.

the size of the property and additional time spent on calculations, research, and mapping.

The seller should have a survey of the property: if so, be sure it was conducted by a licensed surveyor or registered civil engineer; if not, you may require him to obtain one as a condition of the sale, or agree to split the cost. When you seek financing for your purchase, more likely than not, your lender will require a new survey be prepared.

Easements

Unfortunately, sometimes a survey will not show all *easements* that affect the property you want to purchase. An easement is a right or privilege that one party has in the land of another, created by a written agreement. For example, a former owner of the property may have granted an easement to a power company, allowing it to place electrical poles across the land, or to a neighbor whose parcel doesn't have road frontage, enabling him to build a driveway that runs through one of your fields.

Easement agreements are recorded in the permanent land records in the local courthouse and will show up on the *title report* (unless they are "unrecorded," in which case whether or not they are legally binding will be in question) along with liens, *restrictions* (see p. 89), and other matters of record. It is usual to have a *title search*—the review of all recorded transactions in the public record to determine whether anything that could interfere with the transfer of ownership exists—performed by an attorney or title insurance company after you have agreed on terms to purchase the property (see p. 93).

The seller should disclose any existing easements on the land. Utility easements for electricity, telephone, and gas are common; however, they could adversely affect you if, for example, you envision putting board fence along the road for a new pasture, but discover there is a 100-foot right-of-way owned by the electric company. If you inadvertently built the fence—or even your house—within the boundaries of the transmission-line easement, the utility company could legally have the structure removed. In addition, it is wise to ask if the seller has procured, or will procure prior to your purchase, any necessary legal right-of-ways across neighboring parcels to the subject property (for example, an easement on another's property, allowing you to build an access road).

> **SO YOU KNOW...**
>
> ◆ An *encumbrance* is any right or interest in land that can negatively affect its value. Examples include, but are not limited to: easements, outstanding mortgage loans, deed restrictions, and unpaid taxes.

It is a good idea to include a clause in the purchase contract (see p. 91) where the seller warrants the buyer that all known *encumbrances*✦ have been disclosed, giving you legal recourse should a problem arise.

Restrictions

A *restriction*, usually discovered during a title search, is a limitation on the use of a piece of property. It is different from a *zoning ordinance* (see below) because it is established and enforced by a private party rather than the government. You may think you have found the perfect 10-acre tract, but when the original owner subdivided his 50-acre parcel into five pieces, he placed restrictions on each property, including a minimum square-footage requirement on the house built and a rule against keeping large animals (i.e., your horse). In such a case, even if the county zoning office views the land as agricultural, the restrictions of record will override the zoning law.

Restrictions can sometimes be "released" by the seller before you agree to a purchase. If this is not possible and they will hinder your intended use of the property, you may want to look elsewhere.

Zoning Laws and Local Ordinances

Make sure that the property you want to put a contract on is *zoned* for your intended use of the land. Zoning laws and local ordinances control the use of land in a specific area; for example, it can be classified as residential, commercial, industrial, or agricultural. Some zones prohibit horses, and some allow horses, but only a certain number of them, and some allow horses, but do not allow barns! If the property does allow both horses and the buildings related to them, *ordinances* may still dictate the actual placement and construction of your facility. These details are especially important the closer your prospective property is to a developed area. Rural counties that surround a large city can have very restrictive laws in respect to large animals.

Zoning laws and other governmental land and building regulations are not covered in a title report—you must do the research yourself (although a good buyer's agent will help guide you). All zoning regulations are maintained by the town

> **SO YOU KNOW...**
>
> **Note:** in many rural counties, properties zoned as "agricultural" do not require building permits for structures used to house livestock (i.e., your barn).

or county board of supervisors, zoning commission, or building inspector. You should determine the zoning for both the specific property you are interested in and its surrounding parcels. It is to your benefit to have an idea of the area's general direction of development.

Real Estate Taxes

Find out the current real estate tax rates for the parcel you are considering, either through the real estate agent or the county assessor's office. Local taxes will vary, depending on your state and proximity to large population centers. In order to get an idea of the "true" cost of your horse property, it is necessary to figure these in to your new budget.

Rural counties near large cities often suffer from extremely high property taxes because the amount is based on property value as well as local tax rates that support government services, such as hospitals, schools, and street maintenance—both of which increase in areas surrounding dense populations. The tax assessor appraises the *fair market value* (the amount of cash the property would bring if sold on the current market) of the land, often by comparing it to similar parcels nearby that have recently changed hands, and the final tax is determined according to this and the current tax rate.

You may qualify for a "land use" tax break that state and/or counties offer to farmers and those with agricultural businesses. When a parcel is declared "in land use," the owners are charged a much lower tax rate, but depending on the state, there are requirements for participating in the program, such as a minimum acreage of official forestry or specific agricultural plans. There is also a penalty if you ever remove property from "land use" for further development.

Land use is really not a tax *break*, but a tax *deferment*. The state or county will get its money eventually and the rollback taxes can be thousands of dollars, depending on the location and size of the property. In case the property you are considering has been declared "in land use" at some point in the past, it is prudent to check with the tax assessor's office so you are aware of the rollback taxes and can make the seller responsible for them up front. Otherwise, the files could be reevaluated after your purchase, the property deemed no longer used for agricultural purposes, and a bill sent to you for *all* of the tax breaks received on that property over the years.

After you determine the current level of taxation on a prospective property, it is a good idea to estimate future taxes by reviewing how much they have increased in the past few years. Take into account the popularity of the area: the more land being sold around you, the more quickly taxes will increase. The local tax assessor can also give you his own estimate based on the amount you are planning to pay for the property, any improvements you plan to make, and recent sales in the area.

MAKING AN OFFER

Writing a Purchase Contract

When your perfect horse property passes all the preliminary tests, it is time to take the plunge. An "offer" is actually a written purchase contract—this legal document is what eventually binds you to buy the property for a set price, and the seller to sell it to you. Your agent can assist you in deciding what should be included, but the focus is obviously the price and deposit amount you are offering to pay, financing information, and any specific terms of sale you wish to include in the deal. When making an offer, everything is negotiable—you might not get what you ask for, but you can ask. Be specific: if you are willing to pay such-and-such amount if the seller fixes the garbage disposal and leaves you the wheelbarrows and garden hoses, name the terms exactly, and any *contingencies* you have (see p. 92) need to be written into the contract. Once the offer is signed, it is legally binding.

How Much Should You Pay?

Before making a purchase offer, ask your real estate agent to prepare a comparative market analysis (CMA), showing recent sale and asking prices of other properties in the neighborhood. Ask him what he thinks a fair offer would be for the property. This will help you avoid offering too much.

Deposit and Down Payment

The seller not only must agree to your price, but also a *deposit* amount (sometimes called "earnest money")—which demonstrates that you, the purchaser, is acting in good faith and do intend to buy the property. This will go toward your *down payment*, which is the amount of the purchase price you agree to pay up front, in cash, at closing (see p. 96).

Contingencies

It is a good idea to include *financing* and professional *inspection* contingencies within the agreement. These make your purchase conditional upon your qualification for a mortgage and the property's improvements passing inspection. If either of these do not happen, you can cancel your offer and your deposit must be refunded. Contingencies can also include items we have previously discussed, such as satisfactory title report and survey results.

Do not overload an initial offer with numerous immaterial requirements; this will jeopardize the chances of the seller accepting it. Discuss your concerns with your agent to be sure that you do not leave out anything pertinent.

Financing

As I've mentioned before, it is wise to have your credit pre-approved before you go property shopping so you know the mortgage amount you will likely be able to obtain. However, if you do have to shop for a mortgage, you will need to include the terms acceptable to you in your purchase offer. Specifically state the amount of time allowed you for mortgage shopping, the maximum interest you will pay, the type of loan, and so on. Then, you can legally pull out of the deal if the loan you want isn't approved. For more information on the ins-and-outs of financing, see p. 94.

Inspections

Even though you have done your own preliminary walk-through, you should hire a professional home inspector to do a full review of the property, which will include evaluation of structures, electrical, plumbing, heating, chimneys, and appliances, as well as testing for pests, radon, lead paint, and other hazards. There is no limit on the number of inspections that can be requested. Accompany the inspector if you can, bring your notes along, and ask questions about things you may have noticed.

The seller should pay for the inspection for termites and other pests in the buildings (often required by lenders), and water bacteria levels (if the property has a well). However, other inspections are often the responsibility of the purchaser—although you can stipulate a different arrangement in your offer. Fees can run anywhere from $250 to $500, depending on your location and how long the inspection will take. Compare inspection fees, and check an inspector's reputation with the county building inspector or the American Society of Home Inspectors (ASHI) before hiring him.

Be sure to state in the contract that once the various inspections are completed and reports generated, the buyer has the option of asking the seller to fix items of concern. These items will be added to the contract post-inspection via an *addendum*, and if the seller will not agree to fix (or pay for) the items listed, the buyer is no longer obligated to purchase the property.

Additional Terms

It is important to name any item of personal property that you expect to be included in the purchase (i.e., the water hoses and wheelbarrows). This can become a gray area when it comes to things like light fixtures and appliances, so avoid possible disagreements by explicitly stating everything you expect to transfer from the seller's possession to your own.

A right to a final walk-through, and time limits to respond to the offer, close the deal, and for you to assume occupancy should also be included.

Counteroffers and Accepted Offers

After your agent has presented the seller with your written offer, it may be rejected, you may receive a counteroffer, or it could be accepted. A counteroffer means the seller is willing to consider your offer with some changes. These will either be agreeable to you, or negotiations will continue. When both parties sign and accept the final version, it becomes a *ratified contract*—a legally binding document.

Choosing a Closing Agent

An *escrow agent, closing agent,* or "closer," is engaged in the business of acting as a neutral, third party who receives escrows (property deeds and/or purchase monies held in trust until fulfillment of contractual conditions) pending deposit or delivery. You should choose your closing agent as soon as your offer is accepted. He will coordinate and process all of your lender's documentation, including the note and deed of trust, as well as order a title search and binder for title insurance; termite and home inspections, surveys, appraisals and any other items specified in the contract. Your closer also disburses funds upon closing and reports the transaction in the court records.

The closing agent can be a real estate attorney or *settlement agent*. I recommend choosing an attorney; although settlement agents are allowed to perform closings, they cannot give buyers legal advice or prepare deeds. An attorney, on the other hand, can explain documents and provide council, and if along the way you have doubts or questions about the purchase of the real estate, an attorney who is already familiar with you will be on hand—and his advice will have been budgeted into your closing costs. (See also *Closing*, p. 138.)

FINANCING YOUR PURCHASE

Mortgages

A *mortgage* is a loan to cover the difference between the money you have for a down payment on a home, and the actual purchase price. Like many other loans, mortgages are paid on a month-by-month basis, and payments consist of *interest* (the lender's fee for borrowing its money) and *principal* (the repayment of the money borrowed). The *interest rate* varies, depending on the lender, your credit score (see p. 35), the economy, and type of loan, among other things. Obviously, the lower the interest rate, the better off you are.

Mortgages are either *fixed rate* or *adjustable rate*—fixed rates remain the same for the life of the loan, and adjustable rates vary—and they can be paid off over differing periods of time. Traditional mortgages are fixed-rate *and* fixed-term loans: each monthly payment includes both interest and principal, and in the beginning of the loan term, most of each payment goes toward the interest. This way, over time, the amount of principal paid increases as the interest is calculated on a steadily decreasing amount. You can build equity with this type of mortgage.

You might be tempted by an "interest only" loan, offering comparably smaller payments for the first five to ten years of your mortgage—but remember, you are *only* paying back interest in those years! If you have a 30-year mortgage, this means that ten years down the road, you will only have twenty years left to pay *all* the principle—plus interest—so your payments will be larger. I don't recommend this type of loan because you aren't building equity during the first years of your mortgage. If smaller, interest-only payments are all you can afford, you are probably buying "too much house" for your financial situation.

Your real estate agent may be able to recommend a bank, savings-and-loan, or mortgage broker, or you may have to shop on your own for the most competitive rates. Some online services can give you "soft" quotes from lenders, though they don't assist in other areas of closing, such as choosing a settlement agent or title insurer. Do not, however, apply for firm quotes from numerous lenders: each time you authorize a lender to pull your credit report, it lowers your credit score.

Lender Requirements

Many factors will contribute to whether or not you receive the financing you are hoping for, including your income, debt load, credit history, and down payment requirements. You can help prepare for the mortgage application process by getting your personal finances in order *before* shopping for a horse property. (For information on organizing your finances, see p. 21.)

Appraisal

A lender will also require—and usually arrange—an independent appraisal of the property, which the buyer pays for (they tend to be $350 or more). This ensures that you aren't paying too much for the property. According to Joel A. Groover, a real estate agent with Long & Foster Realtors in Richmond, Virginia, "…the appraisal is king, and it is imperative that you have a good appraiser that will work to find comparable properties and will correctly value your property."

When dealing with horse property, appraisers often have difficulty finding comparables: farms rarely have the same number of acres, or the same size and type of house, barn, and riding ring. In the contract, make your offer contingent on the appraisal, and include terms allowing you to request different appraisers or second opinions in case an appraisal does not turn out as you expected. Also define your rights should the home be appraised below sale price (a common clause in a competitive real estate market).

Title Insurance

You will be required to obtain a lender's *title insurance* policy, which protects lenders against loss due to disputed property ownership. In addition, you can purchase an owner's policy, so you, too, are protected against title claims.

Your attorney, lender, or the title insurance company performs the title search that traces ownership of the property and all recorded items relating to it as far back as possible because there could be a problem with the title that occurred long before you considered purchasing the property. Examples of title problems include:

- An undisclosed heir to a previous owner suddenly surfaces and demands his interest in the real estate

- A past mortgage was paid in full, but the certificate of satisfaction (release) was not recorded in the land records.

- A seller was fraudulently impersonated, or a signature forged, at some point during past transactions.

Other items that will appear in the title search are easements and other encumbrances, such as mortgage liens and outstanding taxes (see p. 88).

Title problems may not surface until you are refinancing, selling, or even after you have sold your real estate, but your title insurance policy should protect you even when you are no longer the record owner.

Approved or Denied?

When the lender has all the required information in hand, your loan will either be approved or denied. If you are denied, the lender must explain the decision in writing—you may be able to remedy the problem and be reconsidered.

THE CLOSING

Once the contract is ratified and you have obtained the necessary financing, closing procedures can begin. A *closing* is the act of transferring ownership of a property from the seller to the buyer in accordance with a ratified sales contract. Your closing agent will coordinate and process your lender's documentation, including the note and deed of trust.

Homeowner's Insurance

In order to protect its investment, your lender will require that you obtain and provide proof of homeowners insurance. The minimum amount of coverage will be required, but you may want to purchase additional policies. I discuss different kinds of insurance in depth in chapter 2, p. 39.

"Holding the Title" and the Final Walk-Through

You need to describe the *ownership* of your property, that is, do you own it alone or with your partner?

For example, the most common form of ownership for *married* couples is *tenants by the entireties with rights of survivorship (TbyE)*. TbyE requires both parties to sign on all documents that affect the real estate (and if one spouse dies, the complete ownership of the land automatically vests in the surviving spouse). *Unmarried partners* are usually *tenants in common* (TIC). Basically, each partner separately owns a one-half interest in the property and is not required to have the other party's signature on mortgages, etc. (You can specify *tenants in common with rights of survivorship* if you want the property to automatically vest in the other at one's death.)

If your closing agent is an attorney, he can help you determine the best scenario for your situation.

It is a good idea to stipulate in your purchase contract the right to a "final walk-through." This ensures that the property is in the same condition it was at inspection and that any property agreed to be part of the deal is indeed still on the premises. As a general rule, you should insist that the seller has moved off the premises by closing, and your final walk-through will help make sure this happens.

Closing Costs

Closing costs include everything required to complete the real estate transaction, and are the responsibility of both the buyer and seller. Sometimes, the buyer can negotiate the portions of the closing for which he is financially responsible.

Closing costs can include:

- Real estate agent commissions (usually paid by the seller)
- Property down payment (provided by the purchaser in the form of a cashier's check)

- Title insurance premium and related fees

- Deed recording fees

- Appraisal fees

- Termite inspection

- Home inspection

- Survey

- Attorney's and/or settlement agent's fees

- Loan discount *points* (these are fees paid to lenders to entice them to make a loan by, in effect, reducing the amount they advance to the borrower. Each point equals 1 percent of the loan. They are called "discount points" because they often reduce the interest rate charged on the loan)

- *Loan origination fee* (stated as either points or dollar amounts and paid to the lender by the borrower to cover the costs of issuing the loan)

Signing Papers

At the closing, you will have quite a few documents to sign, such as the note and deed of trust, a "receipt of good faith" estimate and various other forms required by your lender, as well as the *settlement statement* showing the amounts and flow of money from seller and purchaser (fig. 4.1, pp. 100-1). Review all documents before signing and obtain copies of each.

After Closing

Once all documents have been signed, the closer will have the deed and deed of trust recorded in the courthouse among the land records—and you are now the recorded owner of the property. Certain items, such as the *signed settlement statement*, a *home warranty contract* (if you have one), as well as your *owner's title insurance policy* should be delivered to you after closing, and you should call your closing agent if you do not receive them.

I recommend contacting all utilities services in advance so they are transferred into your name, effective on the date of the closing.

Congratulations! You now own your own horse property. Once the boxes are unpacked and you can find your clothes and dishes, you can start enjoying life on the farm with your horses.

A. Settlement Statement

U.S. Department of Housing and Urban Development

OMB Approval No. 2502-0265
(expires 9/30/2006)

B. Type of Loan

1. ☐ FHA	2. ☐ FmHA	3. ☑ Conv. Unins.	6. File Number: 000000011111111	7. Loan Number: 222222233333	8. Mortgage Insurance Case Number:
4. ☐ VA	5. ☐ Conv. Ins.				

C. Note: This form is furnished to give you a statement of actual settlement costs. Amounts paid to and by the settlement agent are shown. Items marked "(p.o.c.)" were paid outside the closing; they are shown here for informational purposes and are not included in the totals.

D. Name & Address of Borrower:	E. Name & Address of Seller:	F. Name & Address of Lender:
John T. and Mary S. Hill 5678 Subdivision Court Your City, Your State 34566	Edward I. and Kay Taylor 1234 Hoofprint Lane Your City, Your State 34566	Mortgages for Everyone 5555 Business Avenue City, State 44528

G. Property Location:	H. Settlement Agent: Jon Q. Attorney	
1234 Hoofprint Lane Your Country, Your State 34566	Place of Settlement: Your County, Your State	I. Settlement Date: December 1, 2006

J. Summary of Borrower's Transaction		K. Summary of Seller's Transaction	
100. Gross Amount Due From Borrower		**400. Gross Amount Due To Seller**	
101. Contract sales price	300,000	401. Contract sales price	300,000
102. Personal property	10,000	402. Personal property	10,000
103. Settlement charges to borrower (line 1400)	4,945	403.	
104.		404.	
105.		405.	
Adjustments for items paid by seller in advance		Adjustments for items paid by seller in advance	
106. City/town taxes to		406. City/town taxes to	
107. County taxes 12/1/06 to 12/31/06	200	407. County taxes 12/1/06 to 12/31/06	200
108. Assessments to		408. Assessments to	
109.		409.	
110.		410.	
111.		411.	
112.		412.	
120. Gross Amount Due From Borrower		**420. Gross Amount Due To Seller**	310,200
200. Amounts Paid By Or In Behalf Of Borrower		**500. Reductions In Amount Due To Seller**	
201. Deposit or earnest money	1,000	501. Excess deposit (see instructions)	
202. Principal amount of new loan(s)	270,000	502. Settlement charges to seller (line 1400)	19,716
203. Existing loan(s) taken subject to		503. Existing loan(s) taken subject to	
204.		504. Payoff of first mortgage loan	150,000
205.		505. Payoff of second mortgage loan	
206.		506.	
207.		507.	
208.		508.	
209.		509.	
Adjustments for items unpaid by seller		Adjustments for items unpaid by seller	
210. City/town taxes to		510. City/town taxes to	
211. County taxes to		511. County taxes to	
212. Assessments to		512. Assessments to	
213.		513.	
214.		514.	
215.		515.	
216.		516.	
217.		517.	
218.		518.	
219.		519.	
220. Total Paid By/For Borrower	271,000	**520. Total Reduction Amount Due Seller**	169,716
300. Cash At Settlement From/To Borrower		**600. Cash At Settlement To/From Seller**	
301. Gross Amount due from borrower (line 120)	315,145	601. Gross amount due to seller (line 420)	310,200
302. Less amounts paid by/for borrower (line 220)	(271,000)	602. Less reductions in amt. due seller (line 520)	(169,716)
303. Cash ☑ From ☐ To Borrower		**603. Cash ☑ To ☐ From Seller**	

4.1 This "HUD-1" from the Department of Housing and Urban Development is a sample settlement statement. The names and amounts depicted are fictional.

L. Settlement Charges

		Paid From Borrowers Funds at Settlement	Paid From Seller's Funds at Settlement
700. Total Sales/Broker's Commission based on price $ 300,000 @ 6 % = 18,000			
Division of Commission (line 700) as follows:			
701. $ 9,000 to Buyer's Agent			
702. $ 9,000 to Seller's Agent			
703. Commission paid at Settlement			18,000
704.			
800. Items Payable In Connection With Loan			
801. Loan Origination Fee %			
802. Loan Discount %			
803. Appraisal Fee to 300		300	
804. Credit Report to			
805. Lender's Inspection Fee			
806. Mortgage Insurance Application Fee to			
807. Assumption Fee			
808.			
809.			
810.			
811.			
900. Items Required By Lender To Be Paid In Advance			
901. Interest from to @$ /day			
902. Mortgage Insurance Premium for months to			
903. Hazard Insurance Premium for 1 years to		500	
904. years to			
905.			
1000. Reserves Deposited With Lender			
1001. Hazard insurance months@$ per month			
1002. Mortgage insurance months@$ per month			
1003. City property taxes months@$ per month			
1004. County property taxes 1 months@$ 200 per month		200	
1005. Annual assessments months@$ per month			
1006. months@$ per month			
1007. months@$ per month			
1008. months@$ per month			
1100. Title Charges			
1101. Settlement or closing fee to		400	
1102. Abstract or title search to			
1103. Title examination to			
1104. Title insurance binder to			
1105. Document preparation to Attorney			100
1106. Notary fees to			
1107. Attorney's fees to			200
(includes above items numbers:)			
1108. Title insurance to Title Company			
(includes above items numbers: 1103,1104)		1300	
1109. Lender's coverage $ 270,000			
1110. Owner's coverage $ 300,000			
1111.			
1112.			
1113.			
1200. Government Recording and Transfer Charges			
1201. Recording fees: Deed $ 250; Mortgage $ 145; Releases $ 16		145	266
1202. City/county tax/stamps: Deed $; Mortgage $			
1203. State tax/stamps: Deed $; Mortgage $			
1204.			
1205.			
1300. Additional Settlement Charges			
1301. Survey to Survey Company		1500	
1302. Pest inspection to Termites R US		150	
1303.		450	
1304.			150
1305.			1,000
1400. Total Settlement Charges (enter on lines 103, Section J and 502, Section K)		4,945	19,716

CHAPTER FIVE

Developing Your Property into a Horse Farm

Now that you have purchased your property, which may or may not include a house (building a residential structure is not within the scope of this book), you will want to improve its use as a horse farm, or turn it into one. Projects and improvements to your property increase its value and appeal. A well-designed, 10-acre estate is more likely to charm a buyer than a 30-acre farm with piecemeal fencing and thrown-together buildings. Besides, being involved in an improvement project can give you a sense of personal satisfaction, and bringing your horse home to a cozy barn that you had a hand in developing will be even more fulfilling.

This chapter is not intended to be a guide for designing horse barns or constructing fences, but rather to make you aware of financial and risk management considerations when undertaking such a building or improvement project.

PLAN YOUR DEVELOPMENT

Before beginning any project that alters the appearance of your land and property—building a barn or run-in shed, or clearing for pasture—create a long-term plan for development. Decide how many horses and any other types of livestock you will have. Do you want a riding ring? Sheds in every paddock? A border of trees for privacy? The back of your property may be tree-covered now, but if a contractor comes in with a bulldozer and you simply instruct him to clear 5 acres for pasture, every tree will be wiped out, and he may clear right to your property line. Suddenly, your back kitchen window might look out at the ugliest house you have ever seen—the one that was conveniently hidden behind all the trees you just cleared.

Everyone has been to a farm or stable that seems disjointed: outbuildings are situated seemingly with no rhyme or reason, and pasture gates put in the most inconvenient places. You want to design your property so that it is functional, easy to maintain, and aesthetically pleasing. By taking your time and creating a "planned property," you are adding to your initial investment and increasing your chances of maximizing your return should you ever sell it.

Contact your local extension agent to help you design the layout of any improvements. Factors will come into play that you may know nothing about, such as soil types, topography, drainage, wetland issues, accommodating existing trees and barriers, and structures on neighboring property. I will touch upon some of these in the following pages.

Fully understand your local zoning ordinances before building anything. There are probably many rules and regulations to follow, from getting zoning permission to required setbacks for location of buildings. Ignore these at your peril! The complications and fines can be expensive. (For more information on zoning, see chapter 4, p. 89.)

FINANCING OPTIONS

Before taking on any improvement project, assess your budget. How will it impact your other financial goals and obligations, such as debt payments, investment plans, and retirement contributions? In the end, a new barn that jeopardizes your financial stability will not benefit you, or your horse.

Construction Loans / Second Mortgages

When it comes to obtaining financing, there are several avenues you can try. If it is for a large project, like a new barn, you can apply for a *construction loan* with a conventional lender. You will usually be required to work with a general contractor the lender approves (and the contractor may have to submit documentation and financial statements in order to be authorized). You will be expected to provide construction plans, documents for title insurance, and any applicable lien waivers (see p. 88). *Draws* (money disbursements) will be controlled by the lender. (See chapter 4, p. 94 for more information on applying for financial backing.)

Another option is to apply for financing from an agricultural lending institution, such as Farm Credit. Generally, these lenders intend to serve people in rural areas with rural lifestyles and so may give you more flexibility in the type, amount, and terms of your loan. Farm Credit can finance many things, including farm residences; barns, sheds, and facilities; horses and other livestock; trucks and trailers; machinery and equipment; and even agricultural business operating expenses (see *Resources*, p. 221).

The interest on mortgages totaling $1,000,000 or less ($500,000 or less if married, filing separately) taken out to buy, build, or improve a home—classified as *home acquisition debt*—is fully tax deductible. A second mortgage or construction loan for improvements to your horse property should fall under this classification, and by deducting interest, you effectively reduce the overall cost of the loan.

Home Equity Loans

If there is already a house on your property and you have enough equity built up, you can take out a home equity loan to cover the improvements (see also p. 34). As long as the debt is secured by your residence, and the sum of the home equity loan and the balance on the primary mortgage does not exceed the fair market value of the property, *home equity interest* may be deducted on a loan up to $100,000 ($50,000 if you are married filing separately). As with second mortgages and construction loans, by deducting interest, you ultimately lower the cost of your loan.

Personal Loan

If you purchased your property recently, you may not have enough equity to use it to finance your project. If you would rather not apply for a construction loan (you may prefer not to hire a general contractor, for example) and still desire tax-deductible interest payments, a short-term option is to obtain funds with a personal line of credit. When your project is completed, you can have your improved property reappraised and then refinance the existing mortgage—or borrow under a second mortgage or home equity loan—to settle your personal loan. While the interest on the initial personal loan is *not* tax deductible, refinancing or taking out a home equity loan would rectify the situation.

CONTRACTORS

If you can finance your project, then you can begin to formulate building plans. Unless you are a capable do-it-yourselfer, this will entail hiring contractors.

General Contractor

You hire a *general contractor* to oversee your entire building or remodeling project: obtain proper permits; hire skilled laborers (*subcontractors*); purchase the materials needed for the job; and meet and satisfy inspectors, as required.

One way to find a builder is to ask owners of barns or other structures that you like who their contractor was and if they recommend him. You can also approach contractors on the job: if you happen to notice land being cleared or graded, or a barn or fence being erected, stop by the work site and find out if the contractor is interested in another undertaking. Check with local lumber yards and hardware, feed, and farm supply stores; employees may have recommendations, and there are often business cards and information posted on the store bulletin boards. Horse magazines generally have classified sections where barn builders are listed, and of course, the phone book is another sensible place to begin your search.

When you have compiled a list of potential contractors, choose a few that sound promising and ask them for references. Determine whether the clients were pleased with the work, if the job was started and completed in a timely fashion, and if the project remained within the original budget. Ask also if the contractor fulfilled all the terms of his agreement and was easily accessible during the construction process. Check with the Better Business Bureau in the area for any complaints against him.

Sometimes, building plans are drawn up by a general contractor after consultation with a property owner, while other times, an architect is used and then "bids" on the project are accepted from several general contractors to find the best estimates. For the most precise bid possible, provide a list of the types of materials and fixtures you would like included. Then when comparing estimates, be sure to note which ones take your specific requests into account; if you intend to have rubber mats in the stalls of your barn, but a contractor doesn't include the price of purchase and installation in his bid, you will end up with an additional cost.

Once you find a general contractor who offers both quality work and a reasonable bid, it is best to sign a written contract regarding your agreement. See p. 109 for more information about contracts.

Self-Contractor

When using a general contractor, you will experience markups on labor and materials—a worthwhile expenditure if your life is already over-scheduled; however, if you have time and patience, you can consider managing the project yourself. With good money management skills and a basic knowledge of construction, undertaking your own improvement project can be a fun, satisfying, and economically beneficial option (with "sweat equity," your cash outlay is lower and your return higher). It can also be frustrating and time-consuming, but if you are aware of the challenges at the outset, you can sufficiently prepare yourself to handle them.

When you are your own contractor, just some of the items you must attend to are plans, permits, materials, and dealings with subcontractors (framers, roofers, electricians, and plumbers)—plus, all the direct finances involved. The finances can be tricky. In order to really save money on materials, you should shop around and take advantage of sales and low prices at large, building-supply stores. But, some subcontractors will only work with materials they are familiar with, so you will have to discuss purchases with them. Your subcontractors will work by contract for predetermined amounts. As you are effectively their "boss," it will be your responsibility to make sure they are doing their jobs and are paid on time. (Note: be sure to have all workers on your property provide proof of insurance—you need to be protected in case someone is injured while on the job.)

I was the contractor for my own barn project, and when I compared my end expenses to the quotes I had originally obtained from general contractors, I had saved 30 percent. With organization, confidence, and a little homework, you, too, can effectively cut building costs.

Subcontractor

As I mentioned, if you decide to be your own contractor, you will need to organize all the subcontractors yourself. Or, even if you hire a general contractor, you may also need a specialized contractor to do other jobs that do not fall under your general contractor's auspices. I have found that in addition to scanning the yellow pages and local advertisements, supply stores are a resource for finding quality people. Building suppliers will usually give you names of contractors with whom they have formed relationships. These will be the people who pay their bills and with whom the suppliers enjoy doing business. For example, I would ask a brick and block supplier for good bricklayers and masonry professionals, and for framers, I would call local lumber mills and companies. A good recommendation benefits the suppliers, too, because you will most likely order materials from them.

Traditionally, it is hard to get contractors to return your phone calls. You may have to call many times to get three good quotes. Bear in mind that how a contractor treats you at this stage is an indication of how he will deal with you after you've signed a contract. If he hasn't returned your phone calls when promised or shown up on time for appointments, more than likely he will handle your job with the same attitude, and nothing causes more trouble than subcontractors who do not complete their work in a timely fashion, according to your agreement. Behavior like this can throw a wrench in the gears of your whole project. If you have ordered the lumber and contracted the labor for building a structure, but the subcontractor responsible for clearing the site is dragging his feet, neither you nor the framing contractors are going to be very happy when the schedule falls apart. It is difficult to gauge how well a subcon-

---

CONTRACTORS AND HORSES

Most contractors don't know much about horses—never mind things like hooves and abscesses. Before any contractors begin work on your property, explain the dangers sharp items can pose to your horses and the importance of picking up nails, screws, and debris as they go. Provide a large magnet and, if you are self-contracting, a trash container. A waste-management and disposal company can deliver roll-away containers to the building site, and dispose of them once they are filled.

If your contractors smoke, designate a smoking area away from any existing buildings and hay/bedding storage, and provide a sand-filled metal pail for all cigarette butts.

Before making a final payment to a contractor, check and make sure the job site has been cleaned.

---

tractor will manage his time. Obviously, factors such as the weather are beyond a contractor's control, but a lack of preplanning or inappropriate prioritization is inexcusable.

CONTRACTS

Whether you have one contract with a general contractor or several contracts with individual professionals, there are items that should be covered in all. The contract should be written and signed by both parties, should constitute the entire agreement (any changes to the contract should be made by written amendment only), and should include the method and schedule of payment. The *contract price* can either be a *fixed bid* or *cost plus* deal: the former states all work and materials in the contract with one total cost; the latter is a pay-as-you-go scenario, plus a percentage profit margin on labor and material costs. Generally, I would not recommend a cost-plus deal as the contractor is not obligated to search for the best material prices or get the job done in the most efficient manner. Without a price-cap it is likely a contractor will be tempted to take advantage of you.

Duties

The duties of each party should be spelled out:

- Who supplies materials?
- What kind of materials are to be used?
- Who obtains permits?
- Who provides the set of plans or technical drawings?
- Can changes or substitutions be made, if necessary?
- Who is responsible for having all of the utilities located prior to work beginning?
- Who must clean up? The contractor should be required to clear the site of all construction debris and trash upon completion of work.

Local Laws and Regulations, and Lien Waivers

The contract should stipulate that all construction should conform to applicable laws and regulations for your locality (see p. 89). Today, most building regulations are based on the *Uniform Building Code*, which provides standards of construction in order to protect people's physical and financial interests. The local building inspector's office can provide information regarding area requirements. During construction, the building inspector will likely make a number of visits to be certain that codes are being properly followed.

The contract should require a general contractor to obtain written *lien waivers* from each of his subcontractors. A *lien waiver* is a signed agreement that states that a supplier of materials or services formally relinquishes all rights to file a *mechanic's lien,* which is a claim filed by a supplier of materials or services against a property in order to seek delinquent payment. Remember, you pay the general contractor, and he is then responsible for paying for materials and for work done by subcontractors. Lien waivers, therefore, will protect your property should the general contractor decide to put off settling a supply bill or withhold pay from one of his workers. If you are managing your own project and you pay all of your subcontractors directly, then lien waivers are moot.

Completion and Warranties

A time schedule should also be included. You and the contractor should specify a completion date, and outline when (or whether) penalties should occur if the work is not completed as stipulated. Often, payment provisions serve as incentives, for example: one-third of the bid is due at inception of work; one-third at a specified point, such as "when trusses are set" or "upon completion of the roof;" and the remaining third at the very end. Only pay contractors according to this agreement.

The terms of the contractor-supplied workmanship warranty should be spelled out in the contract. A good general contractor will fix problems you notice after your project is completed. It should be clearly stated that manufacturer or supplier warranties for any equipment (i.e., hot water heater, washer, dryer) are to be transferred to you, along with applicable operational and service manuals.

Contractor's Insurance

Your contract should stipulate the general contractor has a *commercial general liability policy*, which provides liability, property damage, and bodily injury coverage. He should also provide *workman's compensation insurance* that would pay medical costs and a portion of a worker's income, should someone be injured on the job. Requiring proof of these things in your contract ensures you are not held responsible should an incident occur.

Either you or the contractor can also purchase *builder's risk insurance.* This coverage protects labor and on-site materials in the event of loss or damage. Even if your homeowner's policy covers building materials, more likely than not, the cost of "labor" will not be insured. So, for example, if the contract for your new barn states that labor will cost $12,000, but when the project is two-thirds complete and a fire destroys everything, without the additional coverage offered by builder's risk, you would sacrifice $8,000 in labor—and have to pay it again. (For more information on insurance policies, see chapter 2, p. 39.)

= SO YOU KNOW... =

Tip: contact your insurance agent when improvements, such as a barn or other buildings, are completed to be sure your coverage is increased and thus remains adequate for your needs.

CLEARING LAND

If your project includes clearing for pasture and building a barn, have a professional architect or engineer draw up plans according to your specifications. Or, some barn manufacturers will provide plans for different types of structures and even come to your site and erect the one you choose. Whichever method you use, you need to have your site prepared.

Land Use and Soil Disturbance Permits

When clearing timbered acreage for pasture you may need to obtain a land/soil disturbance permit from your local environmental engineering office. If you are clearing over a quarter of an acre, most localities require a permit, which can range from $200 to $600, depending on your location, and a plan of development.

A simple plan of development that explains you are clearing for pasture and intend to use silt fence to control possible runoff into neighboring properties and streams, and plant grass as soon as you finish grading, will usually suffice. The person you hire to grade should provide the erosion control measures as required, and this responsibility should be stipulated in your contract with him. (Note: you do not require a soil disturbance permit when cutting timber or cultivating the property because you won't be "disturbing" the soil.)

Wetlands

If you have a stream, creek, or wetlands on your property, ask your county's environmental engineering office if these areas are federally protected. If they are, federal law states that nothing within the limits of the *resource protection area* (usually 100 feet from the edge of the protected area—a stream, for example) can be cleared or disturbed, and you—and any contractors doing work for you—need to know where the limits are located. If wetlands are destroyed, the Department of Environmental Quality can fine the responsible party.

Mark Your Property

Your property lines need to be clearly marked for the bulldozer operator and other individuals involved in the clearing process. You want to avoid your neighbor's trees being cleared, incurring subsequent legal and monetary expense. Also, clearly mark with surveyor's tape specific trees you want left standing.

Pasture Development

A contractor with a bulldozer is not going to leave your field ready to be planted. The field must be graded smooth with a tractor and a grader box, then gone over with a root rake to push rocks and sticks to the edge.

It will take at least an entire growing season for roots to develop on freshly planted grass. If you allow your horses to graze on newly established pastures, you will be throwing away the money you spent to have soil tested, limed, fertilized, and seeded. Plan to allow fields at least two undisturbed growing seasons so grasses and legumes have enough time to develop good root systems that can withstand grazing. If you have purchased raw acreage and are creating an entire horse property, create a "sacrifice" lot for your horses until your new pasture is developed, and budget in extra hay for the next two seasons. It can cost over $20,000 to develop 5 acres of pasture, so you want it to be a lasting investment.

Waiting to put your horses into a newly cleared field will also give the land time to settle and reveal any hidden dangers, such as holes. You should walk the field periodically because pine trees, especially, have very long taproots. When land is cleared and trees are pushed over, the holes created by the taproots are initially covered with dirt, but as the land settles, they appear.

You can burn or haul stumps and debris from your site, both fairly expensive undertakings, or you can *windrow*♦ these remains, which is more economical. A windrowed pile of stumps and small trees will rot in four to five years, and then you can hire a bulldozer to spread the pile and haul off any remaining stumps. The rotting pile creates rich compost that can be spread over a large area and you will not lose any soil.

If you plan on burning, a permit is generally required. The permit allows you to burn within a specified time frame and requires the fire is watched at all times.

It takes many years to develop good topsoil. Even long after construction is finished, don't overgraze pasture areas and be mindful of natural erosion and establish control measures to limit it. On hilly pastures, and in areas where water has started to create deep crevices, build simple check dams out of rocks or logs to slow the flow of water. On embankments, lay straw, cloth, or even old hay to help hold the soil until vegetation grows thick enough to prevent further erosion. (Further information on soil and vegetation can be found in chapter 4, p. 84.)

SO YOU KNOW...

♦ A *windrow* is a long row or ridge of heaped material (as if "blown by the wind") usually used for drying hay and grain.

ESTIMATING PROJECT COST

For the purposes of this exercise, let us say you are planning to clear a site and create pasture, erect fencing, and build a barn. What follows are some of the things to consider when determining how much your property improvement will cost.

Clearing and Creating Pasture

A copy of your survey is useful when estimating the cost of clearing and grading for pasture. Mark areas that you want cleared on the copy, and then make a list of other work you want done. For example:

- Timber property
- Burn debris and stumps (or windrow material)
- Grade and root rake field and barn site
- Seed, lime, and fertilize field

You can obtain ballpark figures for seed, lime, and fertilizer for the amount of acreage you are clearing from your local agricultural supply company. When you ask contractors for quotes, make them aware of the specific tasks on your list so you can get accurate estimates, and then compare them to your own figures. Figure the average of these quotes and add the cost of any land disturbance or burning permit fees, then, calculate 15 percent of that total. Add the 15 percent as a monetary cushion and you have an estimate for the cost of your pasture (fig. 5.1).

Fencing

For fencing projects, you need to decide who will be responsible for the labor. There are three choices: purchasing fencing and hiring a contractor to build it; paying the fencing company to do the whole job; or renting a truck (or tractor and trailer) for moving the materials, and a loader or post-hole digger for the holes and doing it yourself. Other things to determine include:

ESTIMATE FOR ESTABLISHING HORSE PASTURE

Land disturbance permit	$ 600
Clearing land with bulldozer ($90/hour x 80 hours)	7,200
Burning permit	100
Operator on site during burn ($90/hour x 48 hours)	4,320
Grading and root raking ($90/hour x 24 hours)	2,160
Lime (1 ½ tons/acre, applied spring and fall)	660
50-50-50 fertilizer (260 pounds/acre, applied spring and fall)	780
Seed (orchard, clover, EF fescue, rye)	500
Subtotal	**$16,320**
15 percent monetary cushion ($16,320 x .15)	+ 2,448
Total amount to budget	**$18,768**

5.1 At the time of writing, an hourly price for equipment operators (i.e., drivers of bulldozers and tractors with implements) range from $80 to $100. The estimated length of time to clear 6 acres (lightly wooded with small, young trees) is from 70 hours to 90 hours; burning stumps and brush, 36 to 60 hours; and grading and root-raking the field, between 20 and 28 hours. This estimate uses the averages of each of these ranges.

- How many feet of fencing? (Your survey, showing the location and length of your property lines, is helpful when determining how much fencing you need.)

- What type of fencing?

- How many gates?

- What type of gates?

Variations of wood fence (post and board); vinyl, which looks like wood; woven wire; and electric tape (tension fence) are just some of your options. Contact your local extension office for charts that compare the different fence types and discuss their pros and cons: durability, safety, maintenance, lasting value, and price. (After two hurricanes and a tornado in 12 months, I gained new respect for Safe-Fence®—see *Resources*, p. 219—a brand of electric-tape fencing. It survived entire trees falling on it.)

Materials, plus labor or equipment rental costs, will approximate your fence total, and add 10 percent as a monetary cushion (fig. 5.2).

= SO YOU KNOW... =

Tip: if you are going erect the fence yourself, here's one way to cut costs further! Before renting any equipment, mark the placement of all post holes with marking paint; then, you can dig all the holes at once. You'll be able to return the equipment sooner, and thus save on rental fees.

Building a Barn

To figure an estimate for a barn or another farm building, distribute the architectural plans to various general contractors for estimates. Add these

---

A NOTE ON TREATED LUMBER

At the very least, all fence posts and support posts for barns and sheds need to be pressure-treated to resist rot. Pressure-treated wood's internal moisture has been replaced with a preservative and has three ratings: *above-ground* use (.25), approved for *ground contact* (.4), or *below-ground/marine* use (.6).

When buying treated lumber, I recommend making sure it is rated for *ground contact*, which is .4. Some of the major home improvement stores use the general label "treated lumber," but the manufacturer's tag on the individual piece of wood states a treatment of .25, which is appropriate for *above-ground* use. If you are not careful, your materials will not be suitable for your project.

ESTIMATE FOR FENCING PASTURE

Equipment rental/one week (skid steer loader and auger attachment)	$1,200
265 pressure-treated posts (4 inch x 4 inch x 8 foot; $4.50/each)	1,200
400 pressure-treated boards (5/4 inch x 6 inch x 16 foot; $8/each)	3,200
2 steel gates with welded mesh	250
2 pressure-treated gate posts (6 inch x 6 inch x 8 foot; $10/each)	20
Ready-to-use concrete (for base of gate posts and corner posts)	70
Galvanized screws (approximately 2,500)	200
Solar fence charger	270
Electric fence wire (approximately 2,120 feet)	70
Insulators (approximately 270 insulators/2 insulated gate handles)	65
Subtotal	**$ 6,545**
*10 percent monetary cushion ($6,545 x .10)	+ 654
Total amount to budget	**$ 7,199**

5.2 This estimate presumes you plan to enclose a 6-acre pasture with three-board, wooden fencing (with one strand of electric wire along top board) and decide to rent equipment and install the fence yourself.
*10 percent is a sufficient monetary cushion for a fencing project as fewer variables can impact cost compared to clearing land or building a structure.

together and divide by the number of estimates, which will give you an average cost.

If you are planning to be a self-contractor, you can instead use the plans to create a "materials take-off," which is a list of items needed to build the structure. Take this list to suppliers for quotes, find the total materials cost, and add at least 10 percent to your materials cost for overage. (Your state's sales tax will be added to materials purchased; however, many states allow an exemption from sales taxes for materials and items purchased for use in agriculture. If you are operating your farm as an agricultural business, contact your local extension office for information.)

Next, contact the subcontractors you will need to perform the work, give them copies of your blueprints, and ask for firm labor quotes. Specify what materials *you* will provide and what you expect the contractors to provide. Compile their quotes. Add the total subcontractor cost to the total materials cost, and you have a building estimate (fig. 5.3).

ESTIMATE FOR BUILDING A HORSE BARN

Materials and labor (total as provided by the contractor)	$13,000
Trash container (dumpster)	400
Two 12 foot x 12 foot stalls	1,200
Stone dust for flooring base	700
Stall mats	480
Stall grills	800
3 buckets	25
2 feed bins	25
2 manure forks	30
2 rakes	25
2 shovels	25
1 wheelbarrow	70
2 sets of cross ties	20
2 bridle hooks	20
2 saddle racks	40
Subtotal	**$16,860**
15 percent monetary cushion ($16,860 x .15)	+ 2,529
Total amount to budget	**$19,389**

5.3 This estimate is for a two-stall barn with a tack room, hay storage area, center aisle, and basic accoutrements, and assumes you have hired a general contractor.

Other items to consider for both general contractors and self-contractors:

- If needed, include the cost of a boom truck to set trusses.

- Include the price of the trash container (dumpster).

- Make sure all the "extras" are included: flooring and stall mats, stall grills, buckets, feeders, feed bin, rakes and pitchforks, wheelbarrows, cross-ties, bridle hooks, saddle racks, and tack locker (just to name a few) are items people need but often don't figure into the cost of the barn.

BUYING MATERIALS

Lumber prices can vary greatly within a year. Gauge the economy and fuel prices—high fuel prices tend to greatly increase the price of lumber and other building materials. You may want to plan your project when material prices are good, though unfortunately, the need for the improvement may dictate its timing. (If you just bought another horse, for example, and winter is on its way, you will need to build that additional stall regardless of the state of the lumber market.)

Obtain quotes from at least five different suppliers. You can often get better prices for lumber from outlying lumber mills than from home improvement stores.

Total Project Estimate

Finally, add the individual estimates for clearing and creating pasture, fencing, and building and outfitting your barn to get your total estimate (fig. 5.4).

RECORD KEEPING

Keep receipts and records of all costs associated with improvements you make to your property. These expenses can be added to the *cost basis* of your home (often your original purchase price, see p. 138). Should you sell your property one day, your profit will be figured by comparing the sales price received to the cost basis. Per the IRS, money spent on additions and other property improvements that will be useful for more than one year—such as putting up a new fence, paving a driveway, or building

	TOTAL PROJECT ESTIMATE
$18,768	Clearing and creating pasture
7,199	Fencing
19,389	Building a barn
$45,356	**Total project estimate**

5.4

a barn—or repairs after a casualty to restore damaged property, *increase* your cost basis. (Regular maintenance, such as fixing a broken window or repainting, does not add value to your home, it simply maintains it.) Deductible casualty losses, payments received for granting an easement or right-of-way, and depreciation allowed if your home is used for business purposes will *decrease* your cost basis. (See IRS Publication No. 17, *Your Federal Income Tax* for further information.)

The amount of money and work involved in establishing your dream farm may now seem overwhelming—like buying and caring for your own horse, it isn't cheap, and it isn't easy. However, with proper planning and careful budgeting, over time, you can develop a fine piece of horse property. Of course, you want to preserve your investment so learning the basics of property maintenance is the next important step.

CHAPTER SIX

Keeping Up the Value of the Farm

YOUR BIGGEST INVESTMENT

Your horse property is not just a place to live and keep your animals, it is also an investment and should be viewed as such. Even if you have no intention of selling your property in the foreseeable future, operate it as if you are planning to sell in five years. Worthy maintenance expenditures will serve you well by not only enhancing your living experience, but by increasing buyer appeal. Items that improve salability are weed-free pastures, quality fencing in good condition (not barbed or high-tensile wire), a fenced riding ring, a well-appointed barn with large stalls and wide aisles, and run-in sheds in turnout areas. Remember, anything that makes your life easier, will make someone else's life easier, too, and a prospective purchaser of your property will realize this.

In some ways, your home is an asset and you are the asset manager. The goal of "your company" is to maximize the return on your assets. It is therefore important to enhance the marketability and resale value of your property by budgeting to keep up with daily maintenance and improve its appeal. A clean, well-kept farm will sell more quickly than a similar farm that has not been cared for, and the faster your property will sell on the market, the more *liquid* your asset. If you remember our discussion in chapter 2, a liquid asset is quickly and easily converted into cash, and therefore of great value in case of a monetary emergency.

In this chapter, I'll touch on the main areas of property management, including those that are often inadvertently overlooked, leading to loss of value.

KEEPING THE PASTURES GREEN

If properly maintained, your pastures can provide a constant source of quality nutrition during the spring and summer months, which will greatly reduce your yearly hay cost. Unfortunately, grazing animals are hard on fields, and a pasture's need for continual care will eventually become evident.

Machinery

A farm tractor is not absolutely necessary to maintain a smaller horse farm—many of the implements you need, such as a drag or harrow and a manure spreader, are designed for use with a small garden tractor. A garden tractor with a 20-horsepower engine and a large mowing deck costs between $2,500 and $3,500. A 4-foot-wide drag or harrow ranges from $250 to $350, and a manure spreader designed for a garden tractor ranges between $600 and $2,000 depending on the size, model, and manufacturer.

However, if you have more than 6 acres of pasture to mow, in addition to lawn areas, a farm tractor can be very helpful. A compact tractor with an engine around 25 horsepower is more than sufficient for a small horse farm or estate. That will handle a Bush-hog, grooming mower, grader box, and a front-end loader. (If you plan to use a front-end loader often, be sure to purchase a four-wheel-drive tractor or you may overstress the front axle.) A 20-horsepower garden tractor is *not* the same thing as a 20-horsepower farm tractor—the farm tractor is larger and much more powerful.

There are many players in the compact tractor market, including Case, New Holland, Kubota, and John Deere, to name a few. A new compact tractor costs in the neighborhood of $9,000 to $12,000, and new implements, such as a grooming mower average $1,300 to $2,000. Used tractors can go from one-half to three-quarters of the price of new ones—if a tractor has a well-built diesel engine, you can buy a used one and never wear it out.

Soil Management

Good soil not only ensures quality pasture, it inhibits erosion and problems with flooding and drainage. An abundance of natural and planted vegetation, and several inches or so of soft, dark, rich-looking topsoil are signs that your property is healthy and fertile. A near perfect soil condition takes a long time to develop, and it is important to realize that maintaining, or improving it is a continuous process.

The soil should be tested annually to ascertain whether your fields are becoming alkaline or acidic. Neutral soils are best for most vegetation growth: alkaline and acidic soils decrease root-growing ability and microorganism activity, which break down fertilizer, thatch, and manure. You might need to adjust the fertilizer, spread sulfur or lime, or add certain minerals to ensure balanced soil that will yield optimum pasture growth.

Soil tests range from $5 to $15 from your local farm supply store or extension office. If you provide your extension agent the results of your soil test, he can determine what you need to spread on your fields, and how often. In many parts of the United States, fields are treated with fertilizer and lime in the early spring and again in the fall.

Often, you can arrange for your local farm supply store to spread fertilizer and/or lime. They can also spray your fields during the summer to help control the weeds that, in some areas, choke out pasture grasses. Again, your extension agent can advise you. The average cost of fertilizing and liming a 5-acre pasture with a balanced fertilizer and 1½ tons of lime per acre is between $500 and $700. Spraying the pasture for weeds should cost between $200 and $350, depending on the chemicals used.

Cutting and Dragging

Cutting the fields regularly inhibits weeds and encourages thicker grass growth. Horses prefer tender new growth—long-stemmed older grasses don't have the nutritional value that fresh growth can provide. Also, most horses will not eat around manure piles or where they have urinated. Dragging the fields with a drag or harrow will spread the manure, causing it to break down more quickly and aiding in the control of flies and parasites.

Pasture Rotation and Manure Management

You can avoid your pastures becoming overgrazed by sectioning off parts for grazing rotation. This also allows areas to be readily available for fertilization via spreading manure.

A manure pile is unsightly, creates a breeding ground for flies, and its smell can cause neighbors to complain. Spreading accumulated manure on your fields will keep your farm looking much neater. Always spread in the pasture—or section of your pasture—that is "at rest" (not currently being grazed). If you have completely bare areas, you can first spread grass seed, commercial fertilizer, and lime, and then follow with the manure, which holds moisture and protects the seed so it can take hold and grow. Eventually, the manure breaks down and becomes soil. (You can also pay to have manure removed from your property.)

Many years ago, spreading fields that were grazed the same year was dangerous because it increased equine exposure to worms. However, advances in health care and the development of effective and efficient paste

---

REINTRODUCING SPRING PASTURE

Horses can colic or founder when suddenly turned out on lush, spring grass, so early in the year, it is important to establish a conservative pasture transition schedule. I find a good general rule during the first week is to allow 30 minutes of grazing per day for the first 2 days, then 60 minutes per day for the next 5 days. During the second week, you can increase turnout to 90 minutes per day for the first 4 days, and then 2 hours each day for the remainder of the week. By the third week, it is safe to increase grazing time by increments of 30 minutes, every other day. See chart below.

Day(s)	Grazing Time
1–2	30 minutes
3–7	60 minutes
8–11	90 minutes
12–14	2 hours
15–16	2½ hours
17–18	3 hours
19–20	3½ hours
21	4 hours

You should cut the amount of grain your horse receives during this transition. Discuss your strategy with your veterinarian. He may recommend a different time frame, depending on the type of vegetation in your pasture.

wormers has reduced the probability of infection. If your horse is wormed regularly and according to your veterinarian's schedule, then spreading manure on your pastures is not a threat to your horse's health. A quality spreader that finely disperses manure will allow you to regraze areas in 3 to 4 weeks, preferably after you have had rain and cut the field again.

Sacrifice Lots

Especially with smaller acreage, it is a good idea to have what is called a "sacrifice lot." This is usually a small enclosed area near the barn that can be used for turnout during the winter months. This allows manure, fertilizer, and/or lime to be spread on large summer pastures and encourages good root growth so the fields can "bounce back" in early spring. When horses are turned out in the summer pasture, the sacrifice lot can then be revitalized with fertilizer, lime, and grass seed.

Avoid Overcrowding

It is unrealistic to expect a 5-acre pasture to accommodate twenty horses—it will be reduced to a dirt lot in no time at all. For pastured horses allow 1½ to 2 acres per horse; otherwise, you will have to be extremely attentive to the state of your fields and rotate your animals accordingly, as well as provide supplementary allotments of hay during the summer.

PRESERVING FENCE

On horse property, fencing must be kept in safe working condition. Broken boards or loose wire can injure a horse, which can mean thousands in veterinary bills, and if your horse should escape and damage another's property, poorly managed fencing can be proof of negligence in court.

Inspect fence lines daily, and repair any breaks as soon they occur. If you use electric wire or tape, even as just a single strand along the top of your board fencing, be especially diligent in dry weather. If not properly maintained, a spark from an electric fence can ignite nearby grass or leaves. This danger can be further avoided by keeping fence lines free from weeds and brush with string trimmers, brush blades, or chemical weed killer. This also makes the fencing easier to access and mend when necessary, and neatens the overall appearance of your pasture.

BUILDING MAINTENANCE

Maintaining the exteriors of your house, barn, and other outbuildings is of the utmost importance because often, interior framework is not pressure-treated, and when repeatedly damaged by moisture, it will eventually rot and need to be replaced. The cost of specialty labor and materials for such projects can run tens of thousands of dollars. Pay especially close attention to any items the inspector may have pointed out when you purchased your property. Though they may not have been relevant to your closing, they could potentially become factors five or ten years down the road.

Pay attention to the interior spaces, as well. Horses can be especially destructive to exposed wood in barns. Horses that "crib" or chew the wood in their stalls are not unusual—the habits usually stem from being bored or cooped-up for long periods of time. I remember visiting a boarding stable where the wall and roof support posts were exposed in some of the stalls. An ambitious horse had chewed one of the support posts he could reach completely through and had started on another. Not only was the structural integrity of the barn compromised, but the horse's stall, and the stalls next to his, were now more likely to give way and possibly injure their occupants. Although $28 worth of angle iron would have protected the exposed edges of the posts, stable management had done nothing.

If your horse is a cribber, I recommend using a "cribbing collar," and put metal grill-work and/or angle iron on the tops of doors and the top boards of stall linings to prevent cribbers and wood-chewers from doing damage.

Do your best to keep vermin and insects under control in both the house and the barn. I recommend regularly examining all structures for wood-destroying insects, such as termites, as well as routinely paying a professional to inspect them. Generally, with treated lumber, you don't have to worry about infestations of wood-boring pests; however, you do have to be diligent in watching wood that is not treated (often used in stalls and tack rooms). Once pests like termites, roaches, bees, and powderpost beetles get into the structure of a building, it can be near impossible to exterminate them entirely, and mice and rats can prove problematic if they discover where the grain and supplements are stored. Consult your local extension agent regarding the particular pests in your area. He can help identify mystery critters and provide advice on how to best deal with them.

Annual Barn Maintenance

I believe it is a good policy to have a checklist of items that are tended to each year, thus instilling a "maintenance habit." $1,000 in basic repairs and upkeep is preferable to $10,000 worth of major rehabilitation.

A spring checklist can include:

- ✓ Wash and reseal (if applicable) the interior of the barn. Every spring, I wash my barn with a 1/3 bleach, 2/3 water solution, let it dry for several days, and then apply a clear sealant (such as Thompson's Water Seal) on all wood. (My horses cannot go inside until everything is dry and the smell is gone.) The sealant prevents pests from munching the wood.

- ✓ Check for wood that looks soft or black, signaling the presence of mold. If you can easily push a screwdriver into the wood, it needs to be replaced. If it is structurally okay, clean it with a 3/4 bleach, 1/4 water solution.

- ✓ Move all stall mats and spray the 1/3 bleach, 2/3 water solution underneath. Smooth out any uneven areas, let dry, and replace mats.

- ✓ Clean the cobwebs from the barn, and as you do, visually inspect wiring for signs of wear or rodent damage. (A good practice is to encase wiring located 6 feet above and 1 foot below ground in a metal conduit.)

- ✓ Make sure all electrical outlets are clean.

- ✓ Clean around light fixtures, wiping off dust and dirt, and replace bulbs. (I have "elevator lights"—light bulbs encased by heavy glass jars and metal grids—so if a bulb blows, the glass and spark, if any, is contained.)

- ✓ Wash and/or reseal/repaint the exterior. For wood-sided barns, I suggest using treated clapboard siding (or similar material). You need to wait several years for treated lumber to accept paint or stain, then clean the exterior using the bleach-and-water solution and stain with a colored sealant. The wood will fade naturally, and you never have to "repaint." Every five years, retreat with preservative.

ENJOY YOUR HOME

The real value in spending money on maintaining and improving your property is that you can enjoy the fruits of your labor. Is it not better to replace the carpet and enjoy it for two years, rather than doing it right before you put your house on the market? And, it makes sense economically, too: if minor repairs to your house, barn, and fenceline are allowed to accumulate, what could have been paid for in small amounts and over a period of time, will end up being a massive project costing a hefty sum.

CHAPTER SEVEN

Selling the Farm

DECIDING TO SELL

Selling property, especially property on which you reside, takes a lot of preparation, effort, and time, and in the end, you don't want to regret your decision. It is, therefore, a worthwhile question to ask yourself *why* you want to sell.

Perhaps your farm can no longer accommodate your expanding breeding business. Perhaps you are retiring and no longer wish to keep your own horses. Maybe a career opportunity requires you to move elsewhere. If you examine your reasons for selling, and it is still the best choice, you need to prepare your home, barn, and land—and yourself—for the market.

YOUR GOALS AS THE SELLER

When you are selling any property, your goals are to *enhance buyer appeal, limit the time your place is on the market,* and *maximize your return on your investment.* These three goals are not mutually exclusive, but all must happen in order to achieve your primary goal of maximum return. When you enhance buyer appeal, the property will move quickly, and you obtain your best price possible. (A property that sits on the market for too long appears "tainted" in the eyes of prospective buyers—it is assumed either that it is overpriced or that something is wrong with it.)

TAX CONSIDERATIONS

It makes sense to maximize your profit from the sale of your property because it is probably one of the best *tax shelters*✦ available. If you have owned a property and used it as your principle residence for at least two of the previous five years, you can enjoy a significant tax break when you sell it. Profits (capital gains) of up to $250,000 for a single person, or $500,000 if married filing jointly, are excluded from tax.

If you must sell your property before you have met these requirements, there are certain unforeseen circumstances that will allow you to qualify for the gain exclusion in the eyes of the IRS, though you may only qualify for a reduced exclusion amount.

MARKET READY?

If you have maintained and improved your house and property during your ownership, you won't need to do much to prepare it for the market. Most real estate agencies have videos and pamphlets available that give you tips: some include decorating ideas and how to arrange the items in your home to have the most aesthetic appeal. It may be a good idea to have an agent visit and look over your farm about a month before you want to list your property. He can provide recommendations on how to increase buyer appeal, usually at no charge.

House

- The *front entrance* to your property and the entrance to the dwelling will both have an enormous impact on the prospective buyer. As he drives onto your property, and then when he enters the house, he forms his first impressions. If they are good ones, they tend to carry through as the rest of the property is viewed. *Neatening the end of the driveway, putting plants out, sweeping the walk, painting your front door*, and *shining brass doorknobs* can enhance the showing of your home.

- Show a clean (windows, too) and tidy house. Invest in a professional maid or cleaning service to keep your house spotless, which also relieves the stress of trying to maintain a showplace and live there at the same time.

- If you have a lot of furniture, rent a storage space and move some of it out while your house is on the market—the rooms will look bigger and more appealing.

- If your walls are filled with pictures and artwork, remove some and expose more wall space. In addition, a fresh coat of paint is a relatively inexpensive improvement that has a significant effect on buyers.

Barn, Pastures, and Riding Ring

- Neatly store all buckets, farm implements, brooms, shovels, and anything else left out of place around the farm.

- Remove cobwebs from barn rafters.

- Replace any blown light bulbs.

- Scrub down the barn: an equal mix of bleach and water works well to clean and brighten older wood, especially in stalls.

- Make sure all stall doors and latches work properly.

- Clean up the paddocks and cut fields, replace any chewed fence boards, and make sure all gates are in working order.

- If you have a riding ring, rake or grade the track and neatly store any training equipment, such as cavalletti or jump standards.

SELL IT YOURSELF OR USE AN AGENT?

Though it is common to see "For Sale By Owner" signs on front lawns, it is important to carefully compare the pros and cons of selling your own property versus enlisting the aid of a professional.

For Sale By Owner (FSBO)

Most often, sellers choose this method to avoid paying real estate commissions, and it can be the most advantageous route if you have an able buyer waiting in the wings. Other sellers simply feel they are more motivated, and know the house and neighborhood better than a real estate agent would, and so therefore can make the better sales pitch.

Realistically, however, selling your property is much more complicated than putting a sign on your lawn and chatting-up interested buyers; you need to be able to handle the business end of the deal, as well. This includes:

- Determining a sale price

- Marketing, including print advertising and scheduling open houses

- Helping buyers with financing

- Dealing with a buyer's agent in negotiations (and paying his commission)

- Making closing arrangements

Successfully handling all of these particulars is no small feat, but if you think you are up to the challenge, I urge you to talk to others who have successfully sold their own properties and read introductory books on the subject (for reading recommendations, see *Resources*, p. 218). Consult a real estate attorney about the pitfalls of self-representation, as well as the specifics of contract negotiations.

The remaining parts of this chapter assume the seller is dealing with a real estate agent.

Using a Real Estate Agent

Enlisting the help of an agent protects your interest in your biggest investment: your property. An experienced professional can ensure that your property is accurately priced, and it is in his best interest to be sure it sells at top dollar. He can also suggest ways to show the property to its best advantage, help qualify buyers, and handle marketing, negotiations, and closing.

Of course, these services cost money. Joel A. Groover of Long & Foster Realtors in Virginia says that today, real estate commissions are typically 6 percent of the negotiated sales price. (The commission is often then split between the seller's agent and the buyer's agent.) It is possible to negotiate a lower fee.

Commission percentage is one factor to consider when finding an agent to represent you and your property (for more information about real estate agents, see p. 79). Ask friends and neighbors who have recently sold homes for recommendations, check listings in the local paper, and surf the Web for local agencies. When you have several agents in mind, meet them and ask them questions to determine their competency and whether or not you would be comfortable working with them. Your list of questions should include:

- How long have you been a real estate agent?
- How many properties have you listed and sold in the last year?
- What kind of marketing plan do you employ?
- Do you have a list of references?

Listings

When you have found an agent you like, you will need to sign a *listing contract*. This is a legally binding employment contract, stating the terms of your agreement with the agent, such as the length of the contract, amount of commission, and special permissions allowing the agent to list and show your property. There are three main types of contracts:

- *Exclusive right to sell* guarantees the agent that only he/his agency is allowed to sell your property: even if you have a colleague to dinner and make the deal over dessert, your agent is still entitled to the agreed commission.

- *Exclusive agency* reserves the seller the right to make his own sale: so if you make a deal with your colleague, you don't have to pay your agent the commission.

- *Open listing* allows the seller to list the property with any number of agents, and then only pay the commission to whomever ends up finding a buyer. (And again, if you make the sale yourself, you do not have to pay a commission.)

PROPERTY VALUE

Your *listing price* should be adequate and in the range of what the market will accept: if your price is too low, then you will not get the profit you deserve; if your price is too high, a prospective purchaser will not be able to obtain financing after the lender's required appraisal (see p. 95).

The best way to determine property value is to study similar parcels near you that have sold recently. A good real estate agent will provide a comparative market analysis (CMA) before pushing a listing price. "The real estate agent should dig to find three good comps (comparable properties) in order to do their homework for pricing the property," says Mr. Groover. "You need comparables when you list the property—otherwise you are not doing your client any good."

A second option is to hire a professional appraiser to help determine the best price for the current market. However, many appraisers won't be familiar with horse property or how to best determine its value. Generally, if you choose a good agent, you won't need to spend additional money on an appraiser.

MARKETING YOUR PROPERTY

The main role of your real estate agent is to advertise and market your property for you. Before listing your property with him, you should have

---

INTEREST RATES AND PROPERTY SALES

Appropriate pricing is one of the key elements to a quick and profitable sale of property. And, when deciding on a listing price, the current state of interest rates must be considered.

Long-term interest rates had been steadily declining for almost twenty years until mid-2004, when the Federal Reserve began raising short-term interest rates to head off inflation. (It is possible that over the next several years, more rate increases could happen to keep inflation in check.) Other rates, including the banks' prime lending rate, are tied to the federal funds rate, so such increases impact consumers.

The years of lower interest rates contributed to the rise in real estate values. Affordable mortgage loans encouraged people to pay more for houses, which spurred a frenzy of refinancing, sales, and purchases. However, as interest rates rise, prospective purchasers will not be able to afford as much, and will again be far more prudent when it comes to investing in land and real estate. For example, at a fixed rate of 6.25 percent, a $350,000 30-year mortgage would cost $2,155.01 per month (not including real estate taxes or insurance). However, at 8.75 percent, the same terms would cost $2,753.45 per month. While approximately $600 may not seem a lot of money, remember that the higher interest rate will affect vehicle payments, credit cards, and other consumer debt, so the effect on a family's pocketbook will be felt at all income levels.

For more about interest rates, see chapter 2, p. 31.

---

some idea of how he plans to do this, and how successful his methods have been in the past.

Because your property is a "horse property," the field of prospective buyers is narrowed to a *target market*. It is best if you can find an agent who is familiar with horses or who specializes in properties like your own, but unfortunately, many capable, likeable agents are just not equestrian-savvy. If this is the case with your agent, educate him by describing what is required of a good horse property and write down what makes your place special—everything from the design and placement of the barn, fences, and gates to your nifty shavings bin with the moveable top for deliveries (see below). A prospective purchaser will remember your property when the agent presents it in a fashion that highlights the special "horsey" amenities.

Print Advertising

With your help, your real estate agent can prepare an information booklet describing your property. Use descriptions that your target market will notice and appreciate. For example:

- 100 foot x 200 foot fenced riding ring with lights, and excellent footing and drainage

- Six-stall barn featuring 12 foot x 12 foot stalls with mat floors, solid partitions, high ceilings, electric lighting, "smoked" windows to allow sunlight but discourage heat, and a stereo system

- Tack room with concrete floor and lockers

- Insulated well pump-house with running water year round

- Subdivided paddocks and pastures, and three-board fencing throughout the property

- Pastures seeded with endophyte-free fescue, orchard grass, ladino clover, and Bermuda grass

- Covered shavings bin with detachable roof for dump truck delivery

- Property includes ideal pond site

How the property is described in advertising is critical. The use of key words is important so potential buyers of horse property can exclude listings that will not be suitable. Further, where you and your agent

= SO YOU KNOW... =

Tip: make sure your real estate agent has a list of items that will not be conveyed with your house and property—they need to be referenced on the MLS listing. (See p. 137 for examples of items that need to be referenced.)

choose to post information impacts response. Using MLS (the Multiple Listing Service) and other Web sites, horse publications, and postings in areas frequented by horse enthusiasts, such as tack shops, large riding stables, and horse shows is imperative.

Showing Your Farm

Your real estate agent will show your property to prospective purchasers. For the sake of convenience, the agent will usually place a lock box on your property with keys and directions to the alarm system (if applicable) inside. Only agents have access to the boxes. Often, a buyer's agent will contact your agent to schedule a time to see a house, and in this case, your agent does not have to be present—he can just give the buyer's agent the lockbox information. With a horse farm, however, it may be a good idea to stipulate that your agent be present each time the property is shown, as he is familiar with the property and animals and can make sure everything is in order after the prospective buyer and buyer's agent leave.

As long as you know your property might be shown, it is in your best interests as the seller to keep it neat and orderly at all times. Remember that a person viewing a prospective home usually tries to envision it as his or her own. Along those lines, put all personal and financial information away and limit the number of personal pictures displayed—you don't want potential buyers to feel as though they are intruding. If you are at home when someone comes to look at the place, make yourself as unobtrusive as possible.

Open Houses

Your agent may want to arrange a weekend *open house*—a day-long "showing" that allows interested individuals to drop by and have a look around. These events are mostly a way to call attention to the property. If a serious buyer does visit during an open house, he or she will likely arrange a private showing for later.

Liability

There are certain characteristics to a horse farm that increase your risk of liability and these items need to be addressed by both you and your real estate agent. During showings and open houses, make sure your real estate agent informs visitors with children that they must not be left unattended. You do not want to be sued because little Johnny crawled under the fence, ran through your field, and got hurt when your startled mare whirled and kicked him.

RECEIVING AN OFFER

Eventually, someone will want to buy your property and will make you an offer. I discuss this process in detail in chapter 4, *Purchasing Horse Property*. As you go through negotiations, keep in mind that only what is *written* is pertinent—oral representations are meaningless when interpreting a contract for the sale of real property.

Go over the offer with your agent: look at the price the buyer has said he will pay, the amount of deposit and down payment, and consider any contingencies, terms, and time limits he has included.

You should already have in mind what you are, and are not, willing to negotiate. For example, a standard real estate contract usually has language that states all fixtures convey with the property. These can include items such as washers, dryers, kitchen appliances, hot tubs, plumbing and lighting fixtures, curtain rods, draperies, ceiling fans, wood stoves, television antennas, satellite dish systems, garage door openers, shrubbery and landscaping, saddle racks, bridle hooks, blanket racks, tack boxes, or really anything that you have to dismantle, modify or unscrew to remove. If you intend to take any such items with you when you move, it needs to be written into the purchase contract, but if you are willing, some fixtures can be useful in negotiations.

Making a Counteroffer

If you agree to the offer with some modifications, make the changes (under the direction of your agent) directly to the buyer's original offer. This will be relayed back to the buyer, who will then accept, or counter again. Obviously, these negotiations can go on as long as one or the other party is dissatisfied.

Once an offer is accepted and signed by both parties, the closing procedures can begin by delivering all related documents and money to a neutral third party: the *closing agent* (see p. 93).

CLOSING

Many things need to be taken care of before the sale of a property can be official—some of which are the buyer's responsibility, and some of which are the seller's. Depending on where you live and the ratified terms of the purchase contract, as the seller you may be required to pay for the property inspection(s), title search, and perhaps some of the buyer's closing costs. For information on inspections, title searches, and closing from the buyer's perspective, see chapter 4, p. 96.

At the closing, the buyer may take his final walk-through to be sure any changes you agreed to make have been done, and any items you agreed to include have been left. If satisfied, he will officially sign his loan agreement, and you will sign over the deed and turn over all keys.

Details

Issues that often take sellers unaware are fine-print contract provisions for things such as home security and satellite dish systems. If you sign a year's contract with a security company and sell your home before the contract is up, you are liable to pay the full amount even though you no longer own the home.

I experienced this problem with a home security company. Though my recently sold farm's new owners were using (and paying for) the same security system, the company wanted to collect the remaining months on the contract they had with me, as well. I was stuck, and to make a long story short, though the company did settle for a lesser amount, I still had to fulfill my contract.

I advise you to use monthly contracts for such items, at least when you intend to put your property on the market. And as my lawyer always reminds me, "read the entire contract before you sign."

At closing (if not before), save yourself trouble and confusion later by arranging to switch all utilities from your name to the buyer's.

CALCULATING REALIZED GAIN (OR LOSS)

When you sell your property, you need to determine how much you made (or lost) from the transaction. This necessitates figuring your *realized gain* or *loss* by comparing the sales price of your home to your *adjusted cost basis*, after deducting expenses of the sale of your home (see also p. 39).

So, the formula is:

Sales Price – Selling Expenses – Adjusted Cost Basis = Realized Gain (or Loss)

The expenses of selling your property can possibly include:

- Commissions
- Advertising fees
- Inspection fees
- Title search fees
- Legal fees
- Loan charges you've agreed to pay for in the purchase contract (see p. 97)

Your property's cost basis includes the purchase price of your home, plus any settlement fees or closing costs you paid *in addition* to the contract price (you cannot, however, include any costs associated with obtaining your mortgage).

The *adjusted* cost basis is the original cost basis *increased* or *decreased* for certain items. *Increases* include additions or other improvements that have a useful life of more than one year, special assessments for local improvements, (hooking up to county water or sewer, for example), and amounts spent restoring damaged property after a casualty. *Decreases* to the basis include deductible casualty losses, payments received for granting an easement, and depreciation allowed or allowable if you used your home for business or rental purposes.

If you are fortunate enough to exclude all gain from taxation (see sidebar p. 130), you generally do not have to report the sale of your property on your income tax return. However, if you do have reportable gains, I recommend consulting a tax advisor the year you sell your property.

The process of selling your horse property does not have to be a difficult one. Employ a good real estate agent with a marketing plan to limit the time the property is on the market and maximize your return on your investment. And, in the end, how you have managed and improved your horse property during your ownership will determine how well the sales process will go.

CHAPTER EIGHT

Starting an Equine-Related Business

There are many opportunities to combine your passion for horses with a potentially lucrative business pursuit. The obvious ways include becoming a veterinarian, or boarding, breeding, training, and selling horses. There are many more specialized occupations, too, such as:

- Riding instructor (traveling instructors, especially, are in high demand)
- Tack shop owner
- Barn- and house-sitting (in-home pet care for hire)
- Equine masseuse, chiropractor, or acupuncture therapist
- Saddle fitter or saddle company representative
- Caterer or concessions manager for horse shows and events
- Equine photographer
- Equine artisan (paintings, jewelry, sculpture, gifts)
- Custom riding apparel designer
- Feed store owner
- Farm services (field cutting, fertilizer spreading, aerating, plugging)
- Hay farmer
- Farrier (blacksmith)
- Equine-specialized carpenter (building cross-country obstacles, barns, stalls, fences)
- Equine broker (assisting in the sale or purchase of horses)

Once you have a venture in mind, determine if there is a market for it—though in many cases, the market will create its own opportunities. For example, you may have heard people express the need for another good boarding stable in the area. Check around: do middle-to-high-quality stables have wait lists for their stalls? Are the field boarding ("rough boarding") stables full, as well? If there is greater demand than supply, the market can accommodate another boarding facility.

With more horse owners purchasing their own farms and keeping horses at home, running equine-associated services is a burgeoning market. Individuals specializing in pet- and barn-sitting, pasture and field maintenance, farm consultation, agricultural supply, carpentry and fencing, riding instruction, and farriery often find more business than can be easily handled, indicating room in the market for more entrants.

A business venture can be both exciting and all-consuming. Take your time and do your homework: assess yourself and the market, and seek professional guidance and counseling. The goal of this chapter is to provide an overview of the entrepreneurial process, as well as a "starting point" if a small business is indeed something you wish to pursue.

SMALL BUSINESS PREREQUISITES

Running your own small business is full of surprises, and if you wish to succeed, you need the skills and personality traits to be able to cope with these proficiently and in a timely manner. Here, I discuss some of the skills I think most necessary.

Knowledge, Passion, and Confidence

Once you have established there is a potential market for your services or products through a comprehensive review of the potential customer base and the existing competition, you should determine if you have the *knowledge* and capability to pull it off. This is the key to success: most small business owners pursue their ventures because they love their ideas, but ultimately, you need to have a quality product, and you need to know your product well in order to sell it. If you are lacking the education necessary, then make the acquisition of it your first priority.

You also need *passion*. You may have been training horses since you were ten years old, but when the going gets tough—whether you're deal-

> ## THE IMPORTANCE OF EDUCATION
>
> Poor training can make a horse mistrustful and difficult to work with, and poor shoeing can permanently damage a horse's legs. If your prospective business specializes in horse training or any aspect of equine health, thoroughly evaluate your knowledge and skill level. Have you studied as an apprentice under a respected professional? Do you have the necessary education to safely perform your job?

ing with a difficult animal, hard-to-please client, or overdue bills—you will need the motivation and drive from a "fire within" to forge on. It is also necessary to be *confident* that you will succeed: your talent and techniques will pacify the problem horse, the client will be satisfied, and the bills will be paid. Have faith in your abilities as a trainer, instructor, or retailer, and wholeheartedly believe that you can make your business work, regardless of trials you may endure.

Financial Skills

Potential capital sources, including lenders and business partners, want to see that you have financial management skills. You need to be able to accurately keep records, track cash flow, report financial gains or losses, pay employees, and handle numerous other tasks that require mathematics. If you need to gain background in this area, attend basic business and accounting classes offered by your local extension service or community college before further pursuing your business idea.

People Skills

Do you have the people skills necessary to survive in business? For example, do you keep appointments? Do you speak well and communicate effectively?

Working for someone else may not be as rewarding as having your own business, but it may be easier. When you work for yourself, you really aren't working for just you. You are *managing* you, but in reality you are *working* for your clients. So, instead of one boss, you may have a hundred of them. There may also come a time when you employ others in your business, and your ability to lead and manage them will be a factor in your ultimate success as an entrepreneur.

MENTAL MODEL

Develop a "mental model" for your business conduct. Give some thought as to how you plan to deal with various scenarios and how you would like others—customers and employees—to perceive you. Then, when you are faced with challenging situations in your business, instead of making spur-of-the-moment, possibly irrational decisions, the mental model may help guide you, thus keeping customer and employee relations at their best.

PURCHASING AN EXISTING BUSINESS

Perhaps you do have the necessary qualities that can contribute to the development of a lucrative small business. If so, what do you do next? If you are lucky, you may find a small business specializing in your niche available for purchase. Boarding farms, tack shops, and equine equipment and riding apparel manufacturing lines are examples of businesses that can be purchased. In these examples, the real estate, improvements, and inventory can easily be transferred from one owner to another. However, for most equine-related operations, success after purchase will depend solely on the expertise and management skills of the buyer: the beautiful barn doesn't make a quality boarding facility—the experienced, conscientious management does. Horse business is one that is built on reputation. It is largely a personal service industry, and trainers, riding instructors, and farriers build their businesses with skill and personality. While it is possible to purchase client lists and pay for educational classes, field experience and client interaction can't be bought.

Purchasing an existing equine business gives you a leg up; however, you still need to develop your own business plan and outline your goals. If you find a particular business you are interested in acquiring, have a CPA knowledgeable in *business valuation* or who holds the credential, *ABV* (Accredited in Business Valuation) determine its fair market, investment, and intrinsic value. This may save you from being taken advantage of and/or paying too much.

Unfortunately, there are very few horse-related business opportunities where existing ventures are available for purchase. It is more likely you will need to start your business venture from scratch.

STARTING YOUR OWN BUSINESS

Financial Assessment

Look at your own personal financial picture. Are your personal finances under control? If your income isn't initially steady, how will you cover your existing monthly expenses, such as the mortgage or the car payment?

Before pursuing your idea further, it is a good idea to assess your personal finances with your future as a small-business owner in mind. Find your current net worth and determine your debt-load (see chapter 2, p. 21). I highly recommend paying off consumer debt (for example, the ski vacation charged on your credit card) before attempting to start your own business. Do you have funds available to invest in your business? If at all possible, put a designated amount of money aside each month as a preparatory cash reserve.

Managing the Risks of Self-Employment

Disability, and Health and Dental Insurance

When taking a financial gamble such as starting your own business, make sure you are adequately insured on a personal level. An accident or illness can be devastating if you are the sole individual responsible for your business; if you get hurt and cannot train horses or teach riding lessons, your bills are still going to be due each month—whether or not you have a positive cash flow. Buy disability insurance in the event you cannot perform the duties required, and also acquire life insurance in an amount sufficient to cover all your debts in the case of your death (see p. 39).

Consider how you will provide yourself (and possibly your family) health and dental coverage. If you do not have a spouse whose employer provides additional coverage, individual policies can be purchased, but are usually quite expensive. Fortunately, premiums paid are deductible for self-employed persons.

Obtaining part-time work that provides health benefits can be a good way to maintain steady cash inflow and insurance coverage while pursuing your business venture.

Retirement Plans

A retirement package offered through your former place of employment can be replaced with IRAs and other plans. Discuss what would be best for you and your business situation with your accountant.

Social Security and Medicare Taxes

When you are self-employed, you are responsible for all your Social Security and Medicare contributions (usually, employers and employees split the costs). One-half of amounts paid can be deducted for adjusted gross income on your tax return, however.

Time-Off

There is no such thing as "paid vacation" when you work for yourself. Often, the self-employed work harder and longer hours than others. To avoid "burn out," you will need to schedule some time for yourself, and your family, to have a break.

Local Zoning and Licenses

Whether you are running a home-based business, or an operation from an outer office, your town, county, state, and the federal government have regulatory requirements that apply to you. It is important to the success of your venture that you do not ignore these, but instead, do your homework and are careful to adhere to the various laws and licensing requirements. Related fines and legal fees can be significant enough to end your business before it even begins.

Check your deed restrictions and your local homeowner's association to see if operating a business from your home is permissible. Contact your local city or town clerk to help you find the right planning office, or call your area Chamber of Commerce, and make sure that the business you are going to operate complies with local zoning regulations. Ask about a business license and what filings you will have to make and when business and property taxes are due.

If you are going to operate under a different name than your own, "trading as" or "doing business as," you will need to file an *assumed* (sometimes called *fictitious*) *name certificate* in your local county office. Again, your city or town clerk can help guide you. Make sure you do not register a name that is similar to another business in your operating area, as that owner could take legal action against you.

Officials will usually find out if you are operating a business without a license or are in noncompliance with local regulations. A dissatisfied client may complain, or some officials even scan local newspaper advertisements for new businesses and independently investigate. Keep in mind, when dealing with local authorities it is better to create a working relationship from the beginning than allow an adversarial one to develop.

Creating a Business Plan

Once you've decided that you are personally and financially ready to pursue starting your own business, your first task is to write a *mission statement* and develop a *business plan*.

The mission statement embodies your long-range goal, or what you want to accomplish in your business. It is the key element of your business plan—the formal document that provides an overview of your venture and outlines the factors that will have a bearing on its success or failure.

The process of creating a business plan—examining the costs associated with going into business and the potential market for your idea—helps you to take a realistic look at what you are about to do. Questions you should ask yourself include: "What is the expected length of time for my business to become profitable?" and, "How long will it take me to build a customer base?"

Further, the business plan will be a critical part of any loan application for start-up funding or money needed for expansion. You can use your business plan to attract investment capital, secure loans, present your venture to potential key employees, and provide proof to the Internal Revenue Service (IRS) that you are operating a for-profit business rather than indulging in a hobby (see *Business or Hobby?*, p. 156).

I have always disliked the terminology "living, breathing document" but that is really what a business plan is: a fluid, continually updated planning tool that can help you stay focused on the future of your enterprise. The business plan can be divided into the following five sections:

1) Description of the business
2) Management and operations
3) Marketing information
4) Financial information
5) Supporting documentation

1) Business Description

Along with your mission statement, you should include a brief description of your proposed venture. Describe your competition. What products and services do they offer and at what price? What will make your products and services different, or more appealing? Provide a synopsis of your expertise and the skills that you will give your business an edge.

Your business description should also include an explanation of the ownership of the business—what the legal structure is (or what you hope it will be) and why it was chosen (see p. 152 for more about these options).

2) Management and Operations

This will prove to be the most important part of your business plan when you are searching for investors and financial support, as a business is often only as good as its manager, or management team. Begin with short biographies of the key players in your proposal: list education histories, qualifications, areas of expertise, and specific management skills.

Explain planned day-to-day operations. Describe key employees, your hiring and screening procedures, compensation plans (payroll service), and your accountant and attorney. This shows you have (or plan to have) support and consultants at your disposal.

Also include a summary of rent or lease agreements and insurance, and a list of prospective equipment and supplies.

3) Marketing Information

Marketing information includes an explanation of the industry in which your business will compete, the product and/or service you plan to offer, and how you intend to reach your market and sell your product.

First, identify your market and the demand for your product or service. Provide information and statistics on the horse industry, locally and nationwide, if applicable. Indicate how many horses are owned in the surrounding counties, and detail the major events, shows, stables, and training facilities—these are both potential customers and competitors. Name the industry leaders and what areas of business they occupy.

Now, how will you reach your potential market? Will you advertise, and if so, will it be cost-effective? What are your advertising goals? Do you have the existing presence in the equine community to attract customers based on your reputation? You will need to market yourself, as well as the product or service that you are offering clients.

Detail and explain the pricing structure you have chosen. Typically, potential clients are lured by better customer service and *lower cost*. Do you intend to be a low-cost provider, or can you convey that the quality of your product is worth extra expense? Research the competitive climate and support your pricing strategy accordingly.

4) Financial Information

It would be foolish to attempt to start your own business without thoroughly researching the financial aspects, and therefore "numbers" are a very important part of your business plan, for your own uses, as well as to show investors and lenders.

In this section, I include a *pro forma profit and loss statement*, which is a projected summary of what you expect your business to both make and spend over a period of time, a *balance sheet* measuring your business' assets and liabilities (see p. 22), and *statements of cash flow* (see p. 28). These should all be estimated over a period of three years, and any assumptions you make (changes in client base, or purchase of more horses or equipment, for example) should be clearly explained.

You should prepare a *break-even analysis*, which shows the point when total sales revenue will equal total costs, to indicate when your business should become "profitable." This will also provide a timeline for you to evaluate your goals in comparison to actual results.

There are helpful computer software programs that specialize in preparing your financial statements, or a Certified Public Accountant (CPA) can assist you. (See also recommended additional reading, *Resources*, p. 218.)

5) Supporting Documentation

Supporting documentation will vary, depending on what stage of formation your business has reached, and/or how much money you are looking to borrow. It may include copies of licenses, legal documents pertaining to the business structure, owners' resumes, insurance certificates, and any written agreements pertinent to the business, such as purchase contracts or letters of intent from suppliers. It may also include personal information, such as tax returns and financial statements from each individual listed as an "owner."

Business Plan Maintenance

As I mentioned, your business plan needs to be continually updated to keep up with the changes your small business will experience. Devoting time to keeping it current will not only help you stay on track, it will prove useful should you need to apply for more funds or show it to an interested investor sometime down the road. J. Elizabeth Amos, a Certified Public Accountant with Mitchell, Wiggins & Company, LLP, says, "It is not enough just to have a business plan. You need to make changes to and modify that plan based on current situations in order to improve your business. You need to show that you are reacting to what is happening in the market." Ms. Amos recommends updating a business plan quarterly.

FINANCING

Start-Up Costs

What are your start-up costs going to be? There are three different areas that will require cash outlay:

1) *One-time expenses*, such as legal and accounting fees, equipment or supplies, inventory—anything you need to "open for business"

2) *Working capital* is the cash you will need to pay everyday expenses and stay open

3) *Reserve capital* serves as a safety net in case of budgeting error or other need

=== SO YOU KNOW... ===

Tip: start keeping expense records as soon as you develop your business idea.

You can estimate the amount of capital your business will need, an important calculation before you venture out and try to find necessary financing (fig. 8.1). Will your business be overhead-intensive? For example, a mobile riding instructor will have lower start-up costs than the owner of a new boarding facility.

From Your Own Pockets—and Your Friends' and Family's

Providing your own funding, or "bootstrapping," from personal savings or credit, or benevolent friends and family, is one way to gain start-up monies. It is often far easier to persuade those familiar with you (and your work ethic) to invest in your idea than outside sources. Should your ven-

ESTIMATED CAPITAL REQUIREMENT WORKSHEET AMANDA RYDER, SOLE PROPRIETOR	
Business license	$ 25
Commercial General Liability (CGL) annual premium	550
Attorneys fees (for review of client release form)	250
Accountants fees (consultation on record keeping)	150
Advertisements in two local papers and one magazine	200
Print fliers and business cards	50
Supplies (paper, daily organizer, ledger book)	70
Cell phone and wireless service	250
Total estimated start-up cost	**$1,545**

8.1 Every business is different, and so is the amount of capital required to start it. Amanda Ryder is an aspiring trainer and riding instructor. At this point in her venture, she doesn't have her own facility or school horses, and so plans to travel to her clients' farms.

ture be successful, this arrangement can benefit all involved, and in the short-term, it offers you interest-free financial support.

Some small businesses are funded with home equity loans or credit cards. Home equity loans are usually offered at very low interest rates, though your home will be on the line if you fail to make payments. Using credit cards can ultimately be an expensive way of obtaining the capital you need and should only be considered if the amount needed is low and you will be able to pay it off in a couple of months.

Outsourcing

At some point, you will probably need to pursue outside funding. There are two types of funding: *debt* and *equity*. In both cases, you need a polished business plan to clearly present your proposal to the lender or investor (see *Creating a Business Plan*, p. 147).

Debt Financing
Debt financing consists of loans that must be repaid, which are generally acquired from familiar sources, such as your bank. There are regular

required payments, and interest is added to the principal. The specific use of the loan and your personal credit history determines the interest rate and other terms. In addition, lenders need to see that you have a large stake in your business, and you need to convince them it is indeed a serious venture, before they will agree to help with financing.

Because banks are businesses too, they are more in the line of financing company growth rather than company start-up—it is simply a safer bet, and the worth your business has already acquired can be considered *collateral*✦. However, the Small Business Administration (SBA) is a federal agency that will agree to guarantee repayment of your loan in the event you are not able. The SBA also organizes Small Business Investment Companies (SBICs)—privately owned firms that lend or invest money in small businesses. For more information about how the SBA can help you, see *Resources*, p. 222.

Equity Financing

Equity financing is money from private investors—individuals ("angels") or groups ("venture capital firms")—in exchange for ownership interest in your business. Essentially, you are "selling" part of your company and now sharing ownership with the investor(s). There is no guarantee that these investors will ever see a return on their money, and of course, if a company fails, they lose their initial investment. Because of this risk, private investors are only likely to commit if they are convinced they will see a favorable return in a few years.

BUSINESS ORGANIZATION

Initially, you will need to decide the type of legal structure you prefer when you create your business plan (see p. 147). However, once you have approached various sources for financial support, you may want (or need) to reconsider your options—for example, perhaps you start out as a sole proprietor, but later decide to form an LLC (see p. 155). Speak with an attorney and accountant concerning liability and tax issues to help you choose the business structure that is right for you.

There are four basic types of business organizations: *sole proprietorships*, *partnerships*, *corporations*, and *limited liability companies (LLCs)*. On the following pages I've included brief explanations of each structure and its tax implications.

Sole Proprietorship

A sole proprietorship is an unincorporated business that is owned and operated by one person. The owner receives all the profits and is personally liable for all the potential financial losses and legal obligations. Profits made are taxed as regular income, and the owner should include Schedule C, *Profit or Loss from Business*, or Schedule F, *Profit or Loss from Farming* with their IRS Form 1040, *U.S. Individual Income Tax Return*.

This is the least expensive, most flexible, and fastest way to get your idea up-and-running, which is why it is such a popular business structure. For instance, if you start giving riding lessons to friends to make a little extra money, you automatically become a sole proprietor.

Partnerships

General Partnership

A general partnership is an unincorporated business formed whenever two or more individuals start a business venture together. Profits and losses are shared by the partners in proportion to their capital investment or as dictated by their partnership agreement. Each partner is responsible for himself, and the other partner(s) in the event of failure or lawsuit.

While regulatory agencies do not require you to file legal paperwork to form this business structure (it can be "formed" with a simple verbal agreement), it is wise to have all involved individuals sign a written partnership agreement specifying contributions, shares in profits and losses, and what happens in the event a partner dies or decides to end his association with the business.

Limited Partnership

A limited partnership consists of two or more owners, with at least one acting as a "general" partner. A general partner has the authority to make decisions, execute documents on behalf of the partnership, and run the day-to-day operations of the business. The passive, "limited" partner(s) do not participate in daily operations and only risk the amount of their financial investment in the company, while the general partner is liable for everything else. Special paperwork must be filed with your state to form a limited partnership and ensure the limited partners' assets are legally protected. Profits are distributed among partners based on the capital investment or partnership agreement.

A partnership, whether general or limited, must file an information return on Form 1065, *U.S. Return of Partnership Income*, and each partner receives a Schedule K-1 (Form 1065) for his or her records. Profits are taxed as regular income to each partner and reported on Schedule E attached to the partner's Form 1040, *U.S. Individual Income Tax Return*.

Corporations

People generally "incorporate" because of business growth and to limit personal liability. The corporate structure is more complex than the sole proprietorship or partnership entities. It is a separate entity, distinct from its owner or owners (called "shareholders"), and can own property, acquire debts, pay taxes, and absorb all legal liability, protecting your—and your investors'—assets. Should the business fail for any reason, the only thing at risk is the stock that owners hold.

To incorporate, you need to file with your state's department of corporations or corporation commission, and be sure you comply with the federal and state agencies that will oversee your company. (I recommend hiring an attorney to help you make the necessary filings.)

A corporation is somewhat expensive to create and time-consuming to maintain, which can limit its feasibility in terms of new, small businesses. Attorney and filing fees can range from $450 to $1,000 for creating and filing your *Articles of Incorporation*.

DIFFERENT NAME—SAME FUNCTION

The state agency responsible for keeping business registration records goes by a variety of names: the Department of State, Secretary of State, Department of Corporations, and State Corporation Commission can all perform the same functions.

There are two delineations made by the IRS of taxable corporations: the *C corp* and the *S corp*.

C Corp

A regular corporation is also known as a "C" corporation because of the tax code. It provides shareholders with limited liability protection, as mentioned. Because it is viewed as a separate entity by the IRS, a C corp's income is, subsequently, taxed on its own. The corporation must file Form 1120, *U.S. Corporation Income Tax Return.*

When a shareholder receives *dividends*✦ from the corporation, those dividends are also taxed as income on the individual's tax return, and a form of "double-taxation" occurs. In a small, closely-held corporation, however, shareholders rarely pay themselves dividends. Instead, they are considered "employees" and receive salaries and bonuses.

> ═ SO YOU KNOW... ═
>
> ✦ *Dividends* are portions of a corporation's earnings distributed as cash to shareholders. Some companies reinvest dividends into the company rather than distribute them, and shareholders instead see their return when their stock increases in worth.

S Corp

If your corporation has fewer than 100 shareholders, you can elect to be taxed under subchapter S of the Internal Revenue Code. The "S" corporation provides liability protection as in a C corp, but in lieu of corporation income taxes, profits pass directly to the owners who declare them on their personal income tax returns. An S corporation must file an information return on Form 1120S, *U.S. Income Tax Return for an S Corporation,* and send Schedule K-1 (Form 1120S) to each shareholder.

Limited Liability Company (LLC)

This unincorporated business entity, created by one or more people, is very similar to a corporation in that the owners are not personally responsible for the company's debts and liabilities. Owners—called "members"—invest in the LLC and receive a percentage of ownership; however, rather than hold stock, as in a corporation—they hold *membership certificates.* In most states, members may include individuals, corporations, other LLCs, and foreign entities. An LLC is the ideal structure for a small group of owners who are active in their business.

The relationship of LLC members is generally controlled by an *oper-*

ating agreement, which is not unlike a partnership agreement. For example, if the members of an LLC want the business to be managed by certain owners, or if they want to employ outside management, they can specify this in their operating agreement. Most states do not require an operating agreement; however, it is prudent to create one for a variety of reasons, even if you are the only member of the LLC. The most important reason is the agreement will help show the courts that you have been diligent in the organization and operation of your LLC, thereby protecting your limited liability status.

One advantage of an LLC is that the member(s) have the option to be taxed as a sole proprietorship, partnership (unless it is a single-member LLC), or a corporation. If you are the only member in an LLC, the fact that it is an LLC is "disregarded" by the IRS, and you can file a Schedule C, *Profit or Loss from Business*, or Schedule F, *Profit or Loss from Farming* with your individual income tax return. Likewise, if the only member of an LLC is a corporation, the LLC income and expenses is reported on the corporation's return (Form 1120). Most LLCs with more than one member file a partnership return (Form 1065). If the LLC would rather file as a corporation for tax purposes, it can elect to do so by submitting Form 8832.

It is relatively easy to convert from a partnership or sole proprietorship to an LLC—which adds to its popularity. All states allow business owners to form an LLC by filing "Articles of Organization" with their Department of Corporations, and the associated fee varies from state to state, but is usually $100. Attorney's fees for creating all pertinent documents, combined with the filing fee for your LLC will range from $700 to $1,100.

To Sum Up

Jeffrey M. Zwerdling, Esquire, does not recommend structuring your business as a proprietorship or partnership because your assets can be lost if you are sued. The liability protection offered by a corporation or LLC is more secure for those starting out, which in the end can make the additional cost, time, and effort involved worthwhile.

BUSINESS OR HOBBY?

The idea for your new small business may begin as your favorite hobby, but it is important that your priorities change to reflect its status as a seri-

Quick Reference: Comparing an LLC to a Corporation

What are the owners of the business structure called?
LLC: Members
Corporation: Shareholders

What provides evidence of ownership?
LLC: Membership Certificates
Corporation: Stock Certificates

Is the business required by state law to keep a list of all owners?
LLC: Yes
Corporation: Yes

Who makes management decisions?
LLC: Members (owners) or specified managers (if it is a "manager-run" LLC)
Corporation: The Board of Directors and Officers

Is the establishment of the entity or the sale of ownership interests subject to federal and state securities laws?
LLC: No (usually), pending all members are active participants in the business
Corporation: Yes, because the issuance and transfer of stock is subject to securities laws. (However, many small businesses are fortunate enough to qualify for exemptions)

How are profits taxed?
LLC: By the individual rates of members (unless the LLC elects corporate taxation by filing Form 8832 with the IRS)
Corporation: At the corporate rate (except in the case of an S corp, which is taxed at the individual shareholders tax rates)

Are the business losses deductible by the owners?
LLC: Loss rules are based on the tax status of the LLC (whether the business is taxed as a sole proprietorship, partnership, or corporation)
Corporation: A corporation may carry forward a loss to offset future income. Shareholders of an S corp may deduct their share of losses but must comply with the IRS tax rules on active-passive loss limitations. Normally, shareholders don't benefit from losses at the corporate level.

ous, profit-making venture. This new outlook will help ensure the ultimate success of the business, both because the work you do will attract new and repeat customers and your expenses will be tax deductible.

Under the Internal Revenue Code, expenses connected with your business activities may either be tax deductible, or if your business will not provide you with "a living" or "make a profit," limited to the rules for hobby expenses. The limit on not-for-profit losses applies to individuals, partnerships, estates, trusts, and S corporations. It does not apply to regular corporations (C corps).

If your enterprise is deemed a hobby by the Internal Revenue Service, that doesn't mean you are not operating a business—you will still need a business license and business insurance (see p. 00). It just means you cannot deduct expenses that exceed your income from the enterprise, and your deductions are further limited by two percent of your adjusted gross income.

The Internal Revenue Service looks at several factors in determining whether you are carrying out an activity for profit. Among them are:

- Possessing the knowledge necessary to operate a successful business

- Operating the activity in a business-like manner

- Depending on income from the activity for your livelihood

- Committing time and effort that indicates your intent to make a profit

- Changing methods of operation to improve profitability

- Making a profit in similar activities in the past

- Making a profit in some years (see below)

- Expecting to make a future profit from the appreciation of the assets used in the activity

An activity is presumed to be operated for profit if it was profitable in at least three of the last five tax years, including the current year. Specifically, equine activities that consist primarily of breeding, training, showing, or racing horses are presumed to be run for profit if they produced a profit in at least two of the last seven tax years, including the current year. The Internal Revenue Service Publication 535, *Business Expenses*, explains the not-for-profit limitations in detail.

Mike Roane, a Certified Public Accountant and partner with Mitchell, Wiggins & Company, LLP, suggests avoiding the presumption of a hobby by keeping a diary of the time spent and work accomplished in your business. Documentation of your efforts, as well as coherent and accurate business records, help prove you are serious about your venture.

BUSINESS INSURANCE

You will need to insure your business, and unfortunately, your homeowner's policy probably won't cover any exposures resulting from a business pursuit.

Liability and Property Coverage, and Business Owner's Policies (BOPs)

Every business should acquire *commercial general liability*, which protects you in case someone is hurt while on your property, or while using your product or services; and *property damage insurance* to cover the physical property you own, rent, or lease, as well as any inventory. *BOPs* are popular packages with small to mid-size businesses, as they generally offer these two types of coverage, as well as compensation for loss of business income or extra expense due to an insured peril.

Supplemental Coverage

In addition to your basic business owner's coverage, there are numerous supplemental types of insurance to be considered. Depending on the nature and size of your business, you may need *errors and omissions insurance*, which protects you against slander, libel, and breach of contract, as well as client claims of error, omission, and negligence. Today, specialized forms of this type of insurance are available for many professions. *Products liability insurance* provides specialized coverage of your liability in case of injury to a buyer, user, or bystander caused by a defect in your product. And, when your business has gained a foothold you may want to consider *theft* and *business interruption insurance*, the former for obvious reasons and the latter to reimburse lost profits in case your business is halted by a random event, such as a natural disaster.

Workers' Compensation

If your business plan includes the immediate or eventual hiring of employees, you will have to shop around for *workers' compensation insurance,* which reimburses for medical expenses and pays lost wages should an employee be injured on the job. Workers' compensation requirements differ from state to state; for example, in some states, if you are a farm employer and have two full-time stablehands, you are required to have workers' compensation insurance. I recommend you contact the appropriate state agency before purchasing a policy.

Key Man Insurance and Business Succession

You can obtain life insurance on "key" people in your organization (the individuals whose absence could cripple your company, such as founders, owners, or integral employees). Should that key person unexpectedly die, *key man insurance* provides the funds to keep your company running while adjustments are made to accommodate new roles and responsibilities, or to allow buyouts during the transition phase.

For instance, if you and your partner are in business training horses together and he suddenly dies in a car accident, you will need funding to hire another trainer to fulfill contracts and obligations, and to eventually buy his portion of the business from his heirs. In this case, key man insurance will provide the money needed to keep your business afloat. An attorney and/or an accountant can assist you in creating a business succession plan and determining how much key man insurance you need.

Reassess Your Needs

Discuss what types of coverage you may need with your insurance agent, and revisit your policies often as your business grows and changes. In the future, you may be able to save money by consolidating or modifying your forms of coverage.

DEALING WITH POTENTIAL PROBLEM AREAS

Cash Flow Management

In order to keep your business going, you need enough "cash flowing in" to pay the bills (the "cash flowing out"). You also need to learn to gauge when you can buy inventory or new equipment (additional cash flowing out) without jeopardizing your ability to pay your employees or vendors in the coming week. A *cash flow projection* can be a very simple and helpful tool in these matters (fig. 8.2).

Inventory

Don't purchase more inventory than you need at one time, and if possible, arrange longer payment terms with suppliers to limit your cash outflow. Slow inventory turnover is a common reason for cash shortages. So, if you are selling horses and you have five for sale and the market seems slow, don't purchase any more for resale until you have moved some of the existing stock.

THREE-MONTH CASH FLOW PROJECTION
AMANDA RYDER, SOLE PROPRIETOR

Inflows:

Receipts from clients	$1,640	$2,500	$4,550
Transfer from savings	1,000	0	0
Total cash inflow	**$2,640**	**$2,500**	**$4,550**

Outflows (what Amanda expects to pay out):

Gas/tolls	$ 228	$ 250	$ 275
CGL insurance	138	0	0
Cell phone	250	55	55
Business license	25	0	0
Advertising	200	150	150
Supplies	70	0	30
Fliers, business cards	50	0	0
Attorney/CPA	400	0	0
Other	0	0	0
Total cash outflow	**$1,361**	**$ 455**	**$ 510**
Net cash flow	**$1,279**	**$ 2,045**	**$ 4,040**

8.2 This is a simple cash flow projection for our aspiring trainer and riding instructor. It only includes amounts related to her business.

Accounts Receivable

Bill your clients promptly, keep up-to-date records, and pursue overdue accounts. If you send billing statements to clients, include language such as "due upon receipt" or "due 30 days from receipt of invoice." Put provisions for late payments, such as interest charged on overdue balances and collection provisions. For example, "A 1½ percent service charge will be added to unpaid balances after 30 days" and "A $35 service fee will be charged on all returned checks" are commonly seen on many invoices. You can also give incentives for quick payment, such as an early payment discount.

If at all possible, avoid extending credit to customers, and if you do, investigate their ability to pay beforehand.

Systems and Software

I recommend using an accounting system that tracks invoices, payments, and outstanding balances. A software package that generates an accounts receivable "aging report," which shows how much is past due and how long it has been that way, can be a true asset. Your accountant or small business advisor can guide you (see *Getting Help Starting Up*).

Acquiring Employees

If your business requires the addition of employees, consult your accountant beforehand to obtain information on what federal, state, and local filings must be made. The United States Small Business Administration and United States Department of Labor may be helpful as well (see *Resources*, p. 222).

It might be best, especially early in your career as an entrepreneur, if you avoid the complexities of payroll and human resource functions by outsourcing these duties to a payroll and/or administration service company, such as ADP or Paychex.

With such a service, you submit employee hours and earnings information each pay period via phone, fax, or the Internet, and the company delivers your payroll and reports to your office, or directly deposits employees' pay into their checking accounts. Mike Roane, CPA, recommends this for small businesses with more than one or two employees. "Payroll services can actually write checks with their own funds, and the client (your business) reimburses them," Mr. Roane adds. "They can be cheaper than having a certified public accountant perform those functions."

An administration company can prepare W2 and 1099 forms for filing with the federal government, and some offer complete tax services to help ensure your company's compliance with local, state, and federal regulations. Complete human resource support can offer important services you may not yet be prepared to handle, such as background checks, state unemployment insurance management, new hire reporting, and compliance documents, just to name a few.

Clients, Friends, and Personalities

You will encounter "problem clients" regardless of the type of business you pursue, from clients who don't pay their bills to those you simply don't like on a personal level. However, business success is based on two main criteria: fair prices and good service. And, although you are not in business to be "friends" with your clients, if you treat your customers as if they are important to you, you will retain them. "Someone told me a long time ago," says Bet Poarch, a well-respected hunter/jumper instructor in Virginia, "that if you treat your customers as if they were your best friend, your mother, or your brother, then you will have no lasting problems."

On the other hand, when "horsey" activities serve as your major social outlet and you go into a horse-related business, you will probably find it difficult to balance business and personal relationships. If you suddenly view all your friends with dollar signs on their foreheads, you'll soon find you don't have many friends left! So, while you should treat all your clients (whether you like them or not) as friends, you should *not* treat all your friends as potential clients.

GETTING HELP STARTING UP

There are many resources out there for the first-time entrepreneur. Your local cooperative extension office is a good place to start (see *Resources*, p. 221). When you explain that you are interested in starting a small, equine-related business, agents will provide you with information on business organization, record keeping, taxation, marketing, and more. They can also give you contact information for other agencies that can assist you.

The United States Small Business Administration co-sponsors Small Business Development Centers (SBDCs) with colleges and universities. There is a central SBDC in every state, and there you can obtain information on developing a business plan, obtaining financing, and record keeping and management issues, among other things. These centers provide economic research for potential and existing businesses, and sponsor counseling sessions and educational workshops, conferences, and courses (see *Resources,* p. 222).

Do your homework first by reading: see the list provided in the *Resources* section of this book. Once you have done your research, meet with your attorney and accountant to discuss your options.

CHAPTER NINE

Contracts

Contracts are a part of life—good contracts make life better, but poor ones can make life worse, so generally, they are not a do-it-yourself project. A contract is enforceable if it can be proven and upheld by a court of law; therefore, if your contract involves a significant amount of money, it should be reviewed by an attorney who is familiar with your state's laws before you, or anyone else signs it.

An *agreement* consists of promises two parties make to one another and is the *manifestation of mutual agreement* between parties by offer and acceptance. When the parties are legally obligated to perform the promises, the agreement becomes a *contract*.

ELEMENTS OF A CONTRACT

There are four elements to an enforceable contract: *mutual assent, consideration, capacity,* and *legality*.

The first element is *mutual assent*, wherein all parties have a meeting of the minds or agree to the promises and terms of the contract. For example, you would like to board your horse at Perfect Stables and the owners of Perfect Stables agree to accommodate you.

The second is *consideration*, or monetary inducement for the parties to enter into a contract. The payment of the monthly boarding fee is your promise to the owners of Perfect Stables and the monthly board fee is their inducement to have you board with them.

The third element is *capacity*, which means a party has the legal ability to make a contract. Mentally incompetent persons, persons under the influence of drugs or alcohol, or minors under the law (under the age of 18 in most states or 21 in some) can rescind contracts after signing, rendering them void and of no legal effect.

The last element is *legality*, meaning simply that the courts can only enforce a contract with legal purposes. You can't contract with someone to rob a bank for you, but you can contract with someone to feed your horse.

Necessary Contractual Items

The following are items that should be clarified in any written contract you sign, regardless of whether for boarding, training, leasing, or transporting your horse:

Parties
The parties to the agreement should be clearly identified with full names, addresses, and contact information. A complete description of the horse should be included, as well as an emergency contact number and insurance information, if applicable.

Effective Date
The contract should be dated when signed.

Promises Made
The contract should clearly describe the *promises, representations,* and *warranties* made by each party. For example, a trainer *promises* that in 60 days, he will have your horse walking, trotting, and cantering quietly under saddle. He *represents* himself as a professional trainer who is qualified to do the job and can offer the services in a workmanlike manner at a horse-safe facility. He *warrants* to you that he is capable of doing the job that you are *promising* to pay him $1,000 to perform.

Consideration
The monetary inducement, or payment, should be clearly described, as well as payment terms, including time and method, late fees, penalties, and remedies.

Commencement and Termination

The contract should have commencement and termination provisions. For example, the training agreement will start April 3rd, when the subject horse arrives, and will terminate after 60 days, or upon request by the owner. With a boarding agreement, termination could be given with two weeks notice from the horse's owner, or the stable owner.

Entire Agreement

The agreement and any schedules attached thereto should constitute your entire agreement. Any prior oral discussions or verbal agreements should be incorporated in the written agreement. This protects both parties from misunderstanding.

Assignment

The agreement should not be *assigned* by either party without prior written approval of the other party. Let's say you are having your horse trained by the head trainer at Perfect Stables, but he overbooks himself, so he sends your horse to Accident Farm to get started under saddle—without your knowledge. If your contract did not prohibit it, he has the right to assign his duties and obligations to a third party.

Waiver

A waiver of a specific term within a contract should not be deemed to be a waiver of the same or any other term or condition on a future occasion. Perhaps you are the owner of Perfect Stables and have stipulated in your boarding agreement that all riders are required to wear safety headgear while mounted. One day, you notice Susie riding without a helmet, but do not say anything to correct her. Just because you chose not to correct her this time does not mean you want it to be construed that riding without a helmet is acceptable.

Amendments

The agreement should only be modified or amended with a written document acknowledged by all parties.

Severability

If any provision of the agreement is to be held illegal, invalid, or unenforceable under any present or future law, then such provision shall be fully *severable* and the remaining provisions in the agreement remain in full force and effect. In other words, if one item in the contract is unenforceable, then the entire agreement cannot be voided.

Liability

Liability issues should be covered in any contract. What each party *is* and *is not* responsible for should be clearly defined.

Venue

This clause determines where any disputes will be litigated. If you have out-of-state clients in your boarding barn, you want any disputes over your agreement settled in your own city, county, or state.

MODIFYING A CONTRACT

It is important to read, understand, and agree to the entire contract you are about to sign. If you don't agree to all terms, a desired modification can be written in, as long as it is initialed by both parties and dated.

For instance, when you go to a doctor's office, you are often given a form to fill out and sign. Generally, this type of agreement says that you are responsible for the bill in the event it isn't covered by your insurance. But, sometimes it may also state that you are responsible for all collection costs, including attorney's fees of up to 40 percent of the amount of the outstanding bill. When I get a form with language like this, I cross through the parts I do not agree with and initial and date the document. In the case of an extraordinary attorney provision as I just outlined, I write "reasonable attorney's fees" in the space provided or specify an amount I'm comfortable with, such as 15 or 20 percent.

Likewise, if you don't approve of a provision in a document pertaining to your horse, ask the other party if you can modify and initial the change in the agreement. For example, you are presented with a boarding agreement that states that your horse must be turned out at all times and is only allowed in a stall during feeding times. If your horse is injured and needs stall rest, this arrangement will not work, so you should modify the agreement to suit your needs and discuss any extra fees that may be involved. If management is unwilling to change, it's a sign you will not be accommodated on other matters that may crop up, either.

Nicole Fox McCabe, an attorney, is a lifelong horsewoman who devotes some of her practice to equine law. She is also the author of "Legal Straight Talk," a monthly column in *Virginia Horse Journal* wherein she addresses readers' legal issues regarding their horses. "Horsemen and women are reluctant to formalize their agreements in writing," she says. "They regard the use of contracts as an insult or an insinuation that a man's word or handshake alone is not good enough. To the contrary, using contracts just makes good business sense and can equally benefit both sides. Although the terms in the contract may initially be in favor of the party that drafted it, the other side is free to make changes that would be more accommodating to their position. In the end, the contract has been modified to meet both parties' needs and both are protected by its terms."

TYPES OF EQUINE CONTRACTS

Purchase and Sale Contracts

This contract protects both the buyer and the seller and prevents misunderstandings involving the transfer of horse ownership. Buying a horse can be exciting, though a stressful event, and a well-written agreement makes the process easier. Along with the basic elements of a written contract, there are several specific items that should be addressed. (See p. 184 for a sample purchase and sale contract.)

Conditions of Sale

It should be specified that the horse under consideration will be inspected by a veterinarian and the results of the vetting must be satisfactory to the purchaser. The purchaser usually pays for the examination (see also p. 11). It is in your best interests to be explicit in the contract to avoid disagreement—for example, if a horse's shoes need to be removed in order to obtain radiographs, declare which party will be responsible for the resulting blacksmith fee.

State that there should be no adverse change in the condition of the horse between the vetting and the close of the sale transaction, and retain the option to reinspect the horse immediately before closing.

Refund of Deposits

A deposit is often used to "hold" a horse until a pre-purchase exam can be arranged (see more information on p. 11). In the event the horse does not pass the vet "clean," you may want to stipulate that your money be refunded, or in the case of a minimal deposit, you may agree that the seller can keep it. Specify the amount of deposit and refund provisions in your contract.

Documents and Breed Registration

Your contract should state that the seller will, in a timely fashion, execute all necessary papers and transfer reports to register the horse under your name as the new owner. Obtain copies of the actual registration papers and transfer reports at the time of the sale.

Time of Sale (Closing Date)

Your agreement should name the time and place that the sale will be final and when the "risk of loss" passes from the seller to the purchaser. To illustrate the importance of this, consider this story of a woman who sold her horse. The buyer paid for the horse in full before he arrived to pick up the horse with his trailer. The horse proved difficult to load (despite the advertisement's claim of "clips, loads, bathes, ties"), and to make a long story short, the horse reared at the trailer entrance, fell over backward, and caught one leg under the trailer. The leg was badly broken, and the horse had to be humanely destroyed.

Because the money had been tendered and the sale agreement did not state specific information applicable to such a situation, the purchaser "owned" the horse and had, therefore, assumed all risk of loss. Ever since first hearing this story, I am sure that my contract states the circumstances and time of sale (when the horse is safely loaded onto my trailer) and I keep the check in my pocket until that time.

Lease Contracts

The following items should be considered when leasing a horse (see p. 187 for a sample lease contract):

Horse Description and Documentation of Condition

A full description of the horse should be provided in the lease. It is a good idea to have a veterinarian perform a "pre-lease" examination—if the knot on the horse's front leg is documented up front, it cannot be blamed on you at the end of the lease. As the "lessee," you should expect to pay for this exam.

Ownership

The lessor should be the sole owner of the horse, and the horse should be free from encumbrances—in other words, the lessor should not still be making remaining payments owed a former owner. The lessor should remain the owner while you lease, and this should be clearly indicated in your contract.

Responsibilities and Insurance

Who will be responsible in the event of an injury to the horse, or if the horse damages someone or something while in the possession of the lessee? Usually, a lease states that the lessor is not responsible for accident or injury to any person, animal, or property during the term of the lease, and the lessee assumes all risk of loss or injury. When a valuable animal is involved, mortality and loss-of-use insurance is sometimes a condition of a lease, with the owner of the horse as beneficiary.

Boarding and Care

The lease should state where the horse can be housed and specifics in regards to his care. The lessee should not have the right to encumber the horse; therefore, he must be careful when signing a boarding contract. If he is unable to pay board for some reason, a stableman's lien could potentially threaten his agreement with the lessor.

Use, Riders, and Equipment

A lease can limit the uses of the horse. The lessor should restrict the horse to activities that he is trained for in order to limit the likelihood of injury or other harm.

A bad rider can mess up a good horse in a very short period of time, so when you lease a horse, it should be to someone you know well enough to be comfortable with his riding ability. The lessee can pledge that, besides himself, only a trainer or instructor who has been approved by the lessor will ride the horse during the period of the lease. In a lease agreement that I used many years ago, I had the following provisions: "Only the lessee and his or her instructor are granted riding privileges.

Lessee does not have the right to assign this lease or to extend riding privileges to anyone. The horse is to be handled and ridden in accordance with the guidelines set forth by the lessor and is to be treated with great care, respect, and kindness. Lessor must approve all tack, equipment and aids used on the horse."

— SO YOU KNOW... —

◆ When something is distributed on a *pro rata* basis, it is proportional to the original amount, according to calculated factors; for example, if you are leasing a horse and have paid for a year's lease up front, but the lessor determines the horse would be better in a different home, it may be written into the contract that fees will be refunded to you, but at a slightly lower rate than the original amount paid. This could be for a number of reasons, such as it might be more difficult to place the horse in December or you may have had the horse for the favored months of competition.

Commencement and Termination

Commencement and termination provisions should be defined in the lease agreement. Does the lease start next week? Or after the equitation finals at the end of the summer? Does it last six months? A year?

The lessor should retain the right to cancel the lease and refund any unearned lease payments on a *pro rata*◆ basis. I recommend that those in the business of leasing horses to clients do so month by month; then, when a rider and horse are poorly matched, you can choose not to renew for the following month.

In some contracts, the lessee has the right to terminate early provided he pays a cancellation fee.

Horse for Sale

Some horses are available for lease with the option to buy, or are simply advertised as "for sale" while they are being competed by the lessee. In these cases, the lessee and lessor may agree on a purchase price at the inception of the contract, and the lessee can then purchase the horse at the specified price when the lease period ends. The contract should state that the horse cannot be sold (to anyone) until the term of the lease is up.

It is possible that a horse that wasn't originally for sale could be put on the market at some point while you are leasing him. In case of this situation, the contract can stipulate that the lessee has right of first refusal. This means that when the lessor receives a monetary offer to purchase the horse, you have the option to match that price.

Boarding Contracts

Boarding contracts are a source of great aggravation for many horse and stable owners alike. There is no one perfect boarding agreement that will fit all parties and circumstances. However, there are certain provisions that should be standard in all, and accompanied by the option of modification to suit individual situations. (See p. 191 for a sample boarding contract.)

Most boarding agreements that I have seen are very one-sided in favor of the stable management. There are numerous provisions detailing the boarder's responsibilities, but few describing that which is expected of management. Keep this in mind when reviewing your boarding contract.

Description of Management and Daily Activities

What is it that management is supposed to provide? Sometimes you see clauses that say, "ordinary care of a prudent horse owner," or "adequate feed and facilities," or "reasonable care." But, who determines "adequate feed" or "reasonable care"—the management or the horse owner? In most cases, it is management. This language protects management in the event it is dealing with an inattentive and ineffective horse owner. However, in the case of a conscientious horse owner, it may leave something to be desired.

I like to have a little more information about what I am getting for my money. The services provided in the boarding fee should be clearly spelled out, as well as the fees for any extra services, and the barn's routine should be clearly explained, and boarders should know who handles their horses on a regular basis. Further, a clear method of communication needs to exist between boarder and management for ongoing services.

Grain, Hay, and Water

Some people like "ribby" horses; however, I like to feel ribs, not see them. To me, adequate feed means my horse isn't bony. Your board fee should include, and your agreement should specify, "X" pounds of commercial grain and "X" flakes of hay per feeding, plus the number of feedings per day, for which management is responsible. It should be stipulated that extra feedings will generate an additional fee, if that is the case. It should be outlined that you want management to provide salt blocks and that your horse should have access to water at all times.

Facilities

What facilities are included? An in-barn stall? Use of the riding ring? At what times? Daily turnout in a pasture? Trails? Cross-country course? These items need to be spelled out.

Leased Space

Does the boarding agreement provide for the lease of a stall that is yours alone, or does management have the right to allow "guest horses" stay there without your knowledge?

Equipment

It should be stated that the owner provides all appropriate equipment for the horse, such as a halter, lead rope, medical supplies, and fly spray. If any supplies are provided by management for "community use," they should be described in the boarding agreement.

Owner's Warranties

The owner should warrant (guarantee) that she is of legal age and the sole owner of the horse to be boarded and/or has the express authority to enter into agreements concerning the horse. The owner should further warrant that the horse is free from communicable disease at the time of arrival. A negative Coggins test within six months of commencement of boarding should be required.

Shoeing, Worming, and General Veterinary Care

The owner is responsible for the cost of shoeing, worming, vaccinations, and veterinary care of the horse. However, the boarding agreement should specify management's right to schedule farriery and veterinary appointments in accordance to the standard of care expected and required at the stable.

Emergency Care

Management should be authorized to secure emergency care, if necessary, for the health and well being of the horse, and for the owner in the event of a fall or other injury. (The latter is especially important if minors ride at a facility.)

Further, if your horse is insured, provide management with a copy of the declaration page of the insurance policy, as well as the insurance company's instructions to follow in an emergency. The fact that your horse is insured and that management agrees to follow the insurance company's procedures should be written into the agreement.

Nicole McCabe, Esquire, had a client whose horse became suddenly, and seriously ill while he was away. The horse was insured, and Ms. McCabe's client had requested management call him in an emergency. Stable management tried to reach him, but failed to connect, and in the meantime, the veterinarian had to euthanize the horse. Unfortunately, the insurance company's procedures were not followed correctly—it was not contacted and did not authorize euthanasia—so the horse owner was not entitled to receive his insurance benefit.

Risk of Loss
The agreement should specify who is responsible in the event of injury, disease, theft, or death of the horse.

Release of Claims and Hold Harmless
The owner should hold the stable, and its employees and agents harmless from any claim resulting from damage or injury caused by the owner, the owner's horse, or the owner's licensees or invitees. For example, a boarder gives a friend permission to ride her horse, but the friend loses control and the horse damages a Lexus parked in front of the barn. The vehicle's owner and insurance company are going to come after somebody—and stable management shouldn't be that "somebody."

Responsibility
The owner should be responsible for and pay for any damages caused by the owner, the owner's horse, or the owner's licensees or invitees.

Assumption of Risks Inherent In Equine Activities
This clause should be in all boarding contracts. It means the owner understands and assumes all risks with respect to horse ownership. Your state's laws should be cited in your agreement.

Property in Storage at Stable
Management should not be responsible for any personal property (tack, equipment, vehicles) left at the stable. Owners should acknowledge that property is stored at their own risk.

Dangerous Animals

Management should specify in the boarding agreement that it has the right to terminate the agreement and request dangerous animals be removed within a specified period of time, such as seven days. Management should have discretion to determine whether a horse is dangerous or inappropriate for their facility.

Remedies upon Default

The boarding agreement should provide for owners who don't pay their board fee, don't comply with the rules of the establishment, and are just generally nuisances. It should outline whether management has a right to retain the horse in the event of non-payment—an "agister's" or "stablemen's lien" is a security interest in the animal to secure the payment of a debt related its care. With proper notification, management has the right to assume ownership and sell the horse in order to recoup unpaid fees. Conversely, the owner needs a remedy against management should it not comply with the terms of the agreement.

Barn Rules

Some boarding establishments have barn rules and fees that are not covered in the boarding contract. These are often posted in the barn by stable management and are subject to change without notice.

The barn rules should be in writing and a copy given to each new boarder. When changes are made, the new rules should be distributed and boarders should acknowledge receipt. It can be very frustrating to drive to the barn one evening after a two-week vacation, tack up your horse and head to the ring, only to find riding hours have changed. Whereas two weeks ago, boarders had unlimited ring access, the rules were changed at some point while you were away, and now, the arena gates are locked.

Barn Hours

Barn hours should be clearly outlined. Owners should have "reasonable" access to their horses at all times—if an owner needs to stay up all night with a sick horse, then he should be permitted to do so. However, in non-emergency situations barn hours should be adhered to. If a boarding facility is at a private home, access to the barn might be from sun-up to 9:00 P.M. (When I had boarders, I allowed 24-hour access provided they telephoned ahead when they were coming onto the farm later than 9:00 P.M.)

Vehicle and Horse Trailer Parking

In order for a facility to operate in a safe and functional manner, designated parking areas are a must.

Guests, Children, and Dogs

This issue will vary, depending on whether a facility is a family boarding stable or a serious training barn. However, for everyone's safety, guests and parents of minor children—regardless if they are riding or just visiting—should be required to sign a waiver and release of liability when on the grounds. Children should never be left unattended.

Dogs should be generally discouraged, or if allowed, should be required to be on a leash while at the boarding facility. Some dogs think it great fun to herd yearlings at high speeds, and some horses think the only good dog is a dead dog (resident barn cats are none too appreciative of strange canines either); so, however nice the dog, it is in the best interests of all that this rule is followed.

Training Contracts

Many of the provisions relating to the care and custody of your horse at a boarding stable are also pertinent in contracts for training, breeding, and other services that require your horse to be away from home. As an owner, you are entitled to know how your horse is cared for and what services are provided. If the contract you are signing is vague with respect to the horse's care, then that clause in the agreement should be modified and expanded. I know this from personal experience.

Many years ago I had a gelding that I had raised from a weanling. He was a delight to work with, and handsome, as well. We had done a lot of groundwork, but unfortunately, I was renting a barn and pasture, and I didn't have access to a safe place to start a horse under saddle. So, I found a trainer. He and his facility seemed adequate, and I was assured my horse would be well cared for and I could visit at any time.

I settled my horse in at the trainer's facility, and five days later, happened to be in the area, so stopped by to check on him. When I walked into the barn, my breath was taken away by the unbearable stench of ammonia. Urine was puddled in the stalls, all of which were bare of bedding. With humidity, the heat index was near 100 degrees and when I looked, my horse's water bucket was empty. Further adding to my horror were cuts on both sides of my horse's mouth, ugly girth sores on his belly, and a huge swelling on one hind leg.

I waited until the trainer arrived. I mentioned I had noticed there weren't any shavings in the stalls, and he replied, "Well, we ran out, but we will get a delivery next week." I then asked how my horse was behaving, and the trainer simply said, "He has been really easy to work with." He offered no explanation for the appalling state of either his barn or my horse. My blood was boiling at this point, and I told the trainer the conditions in his barn were appalling, and I would be back to pick up my horse.

I felt awful; I had betrayed a horse that was intelligent and kind and trusted me completely. I had unknowingly put him in a horrible situation and a signed official document recording our agreement may or may not have motivated this trainer to take better care of my horse, but it would have given me legal recourse.

My horse was eventually started under saddle by a different trainer. (He thought it strange I showed up every day the first week to check on their progress.) My lesson had been learned: when it came to entrusting my horse's care and training to another individual, my expectations and the trainer's promises should be spelled out in the contract.

Standards of Care

Keeping horses at a training facility is similar to a short-term boarding agreement, so review the various clauses in *Boarding Contracts* on pages 172–6. You should feel just as comfortable leaving your horse at a trainer's stable for two months as you would boarding him there for two years.

If you plan to offer on-site training to others, consider the level of care you will be able to provide your clients' horses and explain particulars in your contract.

Training Methods

It should be clear to both parties what training services are to be rendered: do you have a young horse that just needs a solid start, or does your horse have a specific behavioral problem? Do you have a high-head-ed reining horse you hope to compete? An event prospect that's afraid of water? A halter horse that refuses to stand quietly? The specific issue to be dealt with, the trainer's promises regarding that issue, and a disclaimer regarding the horse's future performance should be included. Client and trainer should agree upon a timeline and price.

Specific types of bits or training devices you do not want used on your horse need to be named in the contract. If a trainer says he treats horses fairly and uses resistance-free methods and gentle bits, then these representations should also be written in. This does not mean a trainer won't discipline your horse. If a horse is exhibiting dangerous behavior that warrants disciplinary action, that's okay. (A 1000-pound horse with no respect for his handler is a disaster waiting to happen.)

If you expect your horse to remain at the trainer's facility for the entirety of the training period, it should be made clear. Be aware that assistants and working students may be involved in the day-to-day handling of your horse, and you may want to specify rules regarding their activity, as well.

Horse Shows, Earnings, Winnings, and Travel

Depending on why you are hiring a professional, you may arrange for him to also show your horse. The responsibility for paying the fees associated with showing needs to be worked out in advance. If it is determined that you will pay for your horse's competitive campaign, discuss the schedule of events you agree to be financially responsible for, and outline the expense each entails. Arrange to make weekly (or monthly) payments so your trainer has the cash flow to cover entries, transportation, and stabling arrangements. Along the way, ask your trainer to submit itemized statements that allow you to see exactly where your money goes.

If your horse competes in events that award prize money, it should be stipulated in writing who keeps the earnings, and if they are split, what percentage goes to whom. More often you will need to specify whether you want any ribbons or trophies, or if you want the trainer to add them to his collection.

Your horse will have to be taken to shows. Will the trainer do the shipping in his trailer, and do you approve his transportation method? Read the next section, *Commercial Shipping Contracts*, for an idea of what you should have in writing when your horse is hauled by other individuals.

Commercial Shipping Contracts

The following items should be considered when contracting for transportation (see a sample shipping contract on p. 195):

License

It is important the shipping company you use be legally licensed to "haul for hire" and have operating authority and a number from the United States Department of Transportation. The Federal Motor Carrier Safety Administration (FMCSA) allows you to search transportation companies by number and name, and access current data, including safety and inspection records (see *Resources,* p. 219).

Insurance

Ask if the prospective shipper provides insurance on your horse, and if the company is fully insured for general liability and property damage. If so, request a copy of the certificate of insurance for your records. If your horse is insured, read your policy, or ask your insurance company specifically about shipping coverage. You need your coverage to remain in force even when the horse is not in your possession.

Release Provisions

Carefully read the *release provisions* clause in the shipper's contract. The company should *not* be released for acts of gross negligence.

Vehicles and Trailers, Stops and Layovers, and Health Precautions

What type of vehicle and/or trailer is used by the prospective shipper? Is it appropriate for the distance and climate? For example, if it is late September and you are going to a schooling trial four hours away in Massachusetts, it would probably not be best for your thin-skinned Thoroughbred to travel in an open-sided stock trailer.

Approximately how long will the horse be in transit? If it is a long trip (over six hours), how often does the shipper promise to stop? On trips lasting several days, there should be a layover, and your contract should specify where and how long this layover will be, and in what type of facility your horse will be stabled.

A quality shipper will take additional precautions to protect the health of your horse. Include requirements for leg wraps, blanketing, and a head bumper (if applicable), as these items may need to be removed during a layover or adjusted mid-transit. The contract should state how often the horse will be offered water, and that he will be provided hay for the duration of the journey. (I recommend supplying your own hay to avoid digestive upset during transit.)

Ask whether the prospective shipper requires proof of vaccinations and a negative Coggins test on all horses they transport. Horses being transported across state lines should have a health certificates, signed by a veterinarian, and attesting that they showed no outward signs of infection or disease when examined. Some states also require horses be inspected for brands. Make sure the shipper is willing to obtain all necessary paperwork.

Cancellation

Read the shipper's cancellation provisions. If plans change and you will not be shipping your horse as planned, or if you need to cancel mid-transit because of unsatisfactory service or for any reason, you will want to get all—or most—of your money back.

Breeding Contracts

The following items should be considered when contracting for the breeding of your horse (see examples of breeding contracts on p. 197 and 201):

Fees and Payment Information

In a breeding contract, make sure all required deposits and expected charges are spelled out for you. The "stud fee" is only one of the costs. You also need to factor in mare and veterinary care if you have your mare bred at the stud farm. If you are receiving shipped semen, it should be apparent that the additional costs of the deposit on the shipping container and the price of sending it, and your own veterinary insemination fees, are your responsibility.

Live Foal Guarantee

What is the breeder's definition of a *live foal guarantee*? Some breeders define it as a foal that stands and nurses for at least 48 hours, while others define it as a foal that is able to stand and nurse without assistance within a certain time frame. Usually, a veterinarian's confirmation of either the birth of a healthy foal, or the loss of a foal, is required. Make sure you are satisfied with the contract's definition. If a breeding does not result in a live foal, does the breeder automatically service your mare again? If so, when must the rebreeding occur and what charges and costs are your responsibility? It should be stipulated whether or not the service can be transferred to a different mare, in the case your first mare proves unable to reproduce.

Termination

Should the stallion you wish to breed your mare to be unable to produce sperm, become ill, or die, a clause should ensure that the stud fee and deposits paid are refunded. In this case, the breeder may offer a discounted breeding to a different stallion (or choice of stallions) and these animals should be named therein.

Registration

The contract should state which documents the breeder will execute, and which documents and fees are your responsibility, when arranging to register your foal.

Owner's Warranties

Does the breeder require that the owner warrant that the mare is free from disease and infection? Is the mare required to be up to date with vaccinations, worming, and have a recent uterine culture? A breeder's diligence in these matters is an indication of the quality of care his horses, and therefore your mare will receive.

The items I've discussed in this chapter are just some of the things to keep in mind when contracting for a horse-related activity. These points are in no way a comprehensive list. So, when you plan to lease and board a horse, or board someone else's horse at your farm, sit down and brainstorm. Make a list of your concerns, consult your attorney, and together you can draft a custom contract.

Verbal agreements between friends can quickly go awry due to misunderstanding and miscommunication. "When it comes to agreements, the more that is put into writing the better," says Ms. McCabe. "Having something agreed to in black and white makes it harder to dispute." Even items you think of as basic equine care should be written down. Protect yourself and your horse by making sure the contracts you enter into are clear and comprehensive.

SAMPLE CONTRACTS

The following pages contain a variety of contracts. They are for informational purposes only and *should not be copied for use.* Equine laws greatly differ from state to state, and you should consult an attorney licensed to practice law in your state to draft or review documents for your use.

Nicole Fox McCabe's legal assistance in this chapter has been provided as a reference only and should not be construed by the reader as legal advice. The author and Nicole Fox McCabe, Esquire, will not be responsible for any damages resulting from the use of any contract or agreement contained herein.

PURCHASE AND SALE AGREEMENT

THIS PURCHASE AND SALE AGREEMENT (the "Agreement"), made and entered into this _____day of _____, 20_____, by and between _____, SELLER, and _____, PURCHASER.

RECITALS:

A. Seller is the owner who represents a one hundred percent (100%) interest in

_____

[Breed, registration number, lineage, general description]
_____ ("Horse")

B. Purchaser desires to purchase the Horse from Seller and Seller desires to sell the Horse to Purchaser upon the terms and conditions contained herein.

NOW THEREFORE, in consideration of the mutual premises and covenants contained herein, the parties agree as follows:

1. Seller hereby agrees to sell, transfer, convey, set over and assign to Purchaser, and Purchaser agrees to purchase from Seller all of Seller's right, title and interest in and to the Horse, upon the terms and conditions contained herein.

2. Purchaser shall pay the Seller the sum of _____Dollars, ($_____) as the purchase price for the Horse. The purchase price includes any and all commissions payable by Seller to any agent which may arise out of the transaction, all of which Seller assumes and agrees to pay. The purchase price shall be payable as follows:
   a. _____Dollars ($_____), (the "Down payment"), shall be tendered to the Seller at the time this Agreement is executed by both Seller and Purchaser.
   b. The balance shall be tendered at the time the Purchaser takes delivery of the "Horse" which shall be not later than _____, 20_____. (the "Closing")

3. Purchase of the Horse shall be subject to the following conditions precedent:
   a. Purchaser shall, as soon as practicable, cause the Horse to be inspected by a veterinarian of his choice, the results of which inspection shall be satisfactory to Purchaser in his sole discretion. Purchaser shall have the option to reinspect the Horse immediately prior to Closing.
   b. There shall be no material adverse change in the condition of the Horse between the veterinary inspection and the Closing.
   c. All documents required in this Agreement shall be executed and delivered to Purchaser by Seller and Purchaser shall acquire the entire Horse.

d. The representations and warranties of Seller in Section 6 shall be true and correct as of Closing.

4. Closing will be held on _____ in _____, _____, at such time and place as to which the parties may mutually agree. Upon payment of the Purchase Price and Seller's delivery of the items set forth in Section 5, the Closing shall terminate and risk of loss shall pass to the Purchaser.

5. At Closing, Seller shall deliver to Purchaser:
   a. Certificate of Breed Registration
   b. Bill of Sale and Transfer Report duly executed by Sellers
   c. Such other documents or instruments as Purchaser may reasonably request; and
   d. Possession of the Horse.

6. Seller hereby represents, warrants and covenants to Purchaser as follows:
   a. This Agreement is a valid, binding obligation of the Seller, enforceable in accordance with its terms.
   b. The execution, delivery and performance of the Agreement by Seller, and the sale of the Horse pursuant hereto, do not violate any laws, regulations, orders, decrees or agreements binding upon or affecting Seller or this transaction.
   c. Seller owns good and marketable title in and to a 100% interest in the Horse, which will be conveyed by the delivery of Bill of Sale.
   d. There are no liens, claims, charges, pledges, leases, hypothecations, security or other interest or encumbrances on, against or in connection with the Horse.
   e. Seller hereby agrees to indemnify and hold Purchaser harmless against any and all claims for (i) commissions arising out of the sale of the Horse other than sales commissions incurred by the Purchaser, (ii) the inaccuracy of any representation or warranty contained herein or in the Bill of Sale, and (iii) the failure to perform or observe any of the covenants contained herein or in the Bill of Sale, which indemnification shall survive Closing.

7. Any notice to be given under this Agreement shall be deemed given when delivered by hand, or on the third business day following the deposit of such notice in the U.S. mail, postage prepaid, first class, registered or certified mail, return receipt requested, addressed as follows:

   a. If to Seller:

   _____
   _____
   _____

a. If to Purchaser:

_____

_____

_____

8. Purchaser cannot assign this Agreement without the express written consent of Seller.

9. This Agreement shall be binding upon the parties hereto, their heirs, personal representatives, successors and assigns and shall be construed and governed in accordance with the laws of the State of _____. Jurisdiction and venue for any action arising as a result of this contract shall be in _____County, _____.

10. The parties hereto further acknowledge that the within contract contains the entire agreement of the parties and that neither of the parties hereto is relying upon any verbal assurances of whatever nature that are not contained and expressed in this contract.

WITNESS the following signatures and seals:

Seller:_____ Date: _____

Purchaser:_____ Date: _____

*Courtesy of Nicole Fox McCabe, Attorney at Law

LEASE AGREEMENT

This Lease Agreement entered into this _____ day of _____, 20_____, by and between _____(Herein referred to as "Lessor") and _____(Herein referred to as "Lessee") provides as follows:

1. DESCRIPTION OF LEASED PROPERTY. Lessee has leased this day from Lessor and has received the following property: (Hereinafter referred to as the "Horse") Name: _____ Age: _____
   Sex: _____ Color: _____
   Breed and registration number: _____

2. TERM OF LEASE. The term of this Lease Agreement shall be _____
   (_____) months.

3. PAYMENT SCHEDULE. The first monthly payment of _____ Dollars ($_____) is due upon signing this Lease Agreement. All subsequent monthly payments shall be due on the _____ day of each month thereafter.

4. PERMITTED USES. During the term of this Lease Agreement, the Lessee if permitted to use the Horse for _____. Any other uses of the Horse are forbidden without prior written approval from Lessor.

5. INSURANCE. Lessee shall be responsible for any loss or damage to the Horse. Lessee agrees to purchase the following insurance coverages (i.e. mortality, major medical and surgical, liability) during the terms of this Lease Agreement:

   _____
   _____
   _____
   _____

   Subject to the Lessor's right to reject an insurance company or agent on the basis of reasonable standards, uniformly applied, Lessee will buy the required insurance coverages from an insurance company of his/her choice.

6. MAINTENANCE. Lessee shall be responsible for all maintenance and care of the Horse, to include but not limited to, boarding fees, transport and travel fees, food, hay and medication costs, farrier and veterinary bills and any and all other expenses incurred for the daily care and proper maintenance of said Horse.

7. RISK OF LOSS. As between Lessee and Lessor, Lessee shall be responsible for any loss, theft, or damage to, the Horse (collectively "Loss") from any cause at all, whether or not insured, until it is delivered to Lessor at the end of this Lease. Unless this Lease is otherwise terminated for reasons stated herein, Lessee is required to make all Lease payments even if there is a Loss. Lessee must notify Lessor immediately, both by telephone and in writing, of any Loss.

8. STANDARD OF CARE. The Horse is to be treated and cared for at all times in the same manner and likeness as it is accustomed and as a reasonable person would care for the Horse in its condition. In the event that Lessor, in his/her own discretion, feels that the Horse is not being properly cared for, the Lessor shall have the right to terminate this Lease Agreement and take immediate possession of the Horse. Lessor shall have the right, in the event of Lessee's failure to properly care for Horse, to enter upon any property where the Horse is located in order to repossess it.

9. CONDITION OF HORSE. Lessor has expressly made Lessee aware of the following condition of the Horse:

    _____.

    As a result of this condition, Horse requires a higher standard of care and medical treatment in the form of:_____.
    Lessee acknowledges and accepts the Horse in this condition and expressly agrees to continue to treat this condition with the proper medication and financially provide for such treatment.

10. RELEASE OF LIABILITY. By entering into this contract with Lessor, Lessee expressly waives his/her rights to sue or maintain an action against, or recover from, Lessor for any injury to or death of Lessee as a result of any actions of the Horse and Lessee further agrees to assume all risks specifically enumerated herein: [Cite language from State's liability law, as applicable]

11. INDEMNIFICATION. Lessee shall hold Lessor harmless and indemnify Lessor against any claim and/or liability, loss or expense whatsoever, including attorney's fees and the costs of defense, arising out of the maintenance, use, condition, transportation, possession, repossession, or ownership of the Horse during the term of this Lease.

12. REMEDIES UPON DEFAULT. If Lessee is in default, Lessor shall have the right to terminate this Lease Agreement and take immediate possession of the Horse. Lessor shall have the right, in the event of default to enter upon any property where the Horse is located in order to repossess it.

13. EARLY TERMINATION. Either party may terminate this Lease Agreement without cause before the scheduled end of its term by providing the other party a written notice at least thirty days in advance of the termination date. Any expenses incurred as a direct result of the early termination will be the responsibility of the party who wishes to terminate the Lease Agreement.

14. RETURN OF THE HORSE. At the scheduled end of the Lease Term or as otherwise terminated herein, Lessee shall return the Horse to Lessor at_____, or otherwise as Lessor may direct. All expenses associated

with the return of the Horse will be the responsibility of the Lessee. If Lessee retains possession of the Horse beyond the scheduled end of the Lease Term, Lessee shall continue to pay according to the terms of this lease. Payments by the Lessee beyond the scheduled end of the Lease term shall not entitle the Lessee to retain the Horse, unless other arrangements are made and agreed to by the parties in writing.

15. DAMAGE TO HORSE. Lessee shall be responsible for all damage to the Horse and its loss or destruction from any cause. Lessee shall immediately notify Lessor and Lessee's insurance carrier of any damage, loss or destruction. Lessee shall cooperate with any investigation by Lessor or by any insurance company or police agency as to any damage, loss or destruction of the horse.

16. DISCLAIMER OF WARRANTY. Lessee and Lessor hereby agree that there are no express warranties given pertaining to the Horse. Lessee accepts the Horse from Lessor "As Is" with all conditions listed in paragraph 9 above. Lessor hereby disclaims any express warranties and any implied warranties of merchantability, fitness for any particular purpose, or any other implied warranty.

17. NOTICES. Lessee shall notify Lessor in writing within ten (10) days of any change of address or change of location of the Horse. Any notice from Lessor to Lessee shall be deemed sufficient if sent by regular mail to the last stated address of the Lessee.

18. LOCATION OF THE HORSE. Lessee shall not remove the Horse from the State of _____ without prior written consent of the Lessor.

19. LIABILITY OF ALL LESSEES. All parties signing this Lease Agreement as "Lessees" shall be jointly and severally liable for all obligations imposed by this Lease Agreement on Lessee.

20. NO MODIFICATION. This Lease Agreement sets forth the full and final agreement between the Lessor and Lessee. There are no other agreements. This Lease Agreement can only be modified by a writing signed by both Lessor and Lessee.

21. GOVERNING LAW AND SEVERABILITY. This Lease Agreement shall be interpreted and governed under the laws of the State of _____. If any portion or provision of this Lease Agreement shall be adjudged invalid, illegal or unenforceable, no other provision shall be affected in any way.

22. CUMULATION OF RIGHTS. All rights of Lessor are cumulative and its taking any action shall not be a bar to Lessor taking any other action. Any forbearance by Lessor in taking any action hereunder in one instance shall not be deemed a waiver to enforce its rights in any other similar occurrence.

WITNESS the following signatures and seals:

_____   _____
Lessor   Date

_____   _____
Lessor   Date

_____   _____
Lessee   Date

_____   _____
Lessee   Date

*Courtesy of Nicole Fox McCabe, Attorney at Law

BOARDING AGREEMENT

THIS BOARDING AGREEMENT, made and entered into this _____day of
_____, 20___, by and between _____, hereinafter referred to
as "Operators" and _____whose address is
_____, hereinafter referred to as "Owner".

WITNESSETH:

    (A) The Operators operate _____, which is a stable located at
        _____ in _____ and they are engaged in the
        business of boarding horses thereon.

    (B) The Owner is the owner of the horse or horses more particularly described below:

Name _____	Name _____
Age _____	Age _____
Color _____	Color _____
Breed _____	Breed _____
Sex _____	Sex _____
Registration # _____	Registration # _____
Markings _____	Markings _____

NOW THEREFORE, for good and valuable consideration, the parties hereby agree as follows:

1. Subject to the terms and conditions hereinafter set forth, and in consideration of
    the sum of $_____, per month, per horse, paid by Owner to Operators on
    the first day of each month, Operators agree to board the herein described horse(s)
    at their stable commencing on _____. A late fee of $_____ will be
    assessed if the payment is not received by the fifth day of the month.

2. Operators agree to provide adequate feed and facilities for normal and reasonable
    care required to maintain the health and well being of the animal(s). Operators
    will provide a minimum stall size for each horse, _____in size.

3. Owner shall be solely responsible for the exercise of the animal(s) and it is express-
    ly understood by the Owner that the horse(s) will/will not be turned out by the
    Operators.

4. During the time that the horse(s) is/are in custody of Operators, Operators shall
    not be liable for any sickness, disease, theft, running away, death or injury which
    may be suffered by the horse or any other cause of action, whatsoever, arising out
    of or being connected in any way with the boarding of said horse(s). This
    includes, but is not limited to any personal injury or disability the Owner may
    receive while on the Operators' premises. Pursuant to [cite State's Liability Law if
    applicable]

5. The Owner fully understands that the Operators do not carry insurance on any horses not owned by them, for boarding or any other purposes, for which the horse(s) are covered under any public liability, accidental injury, theft or equine mortality insurance and all the risks connected with the boarding or for any other reason for which the horse(s) is/are in possession on the premises of Operators, are to be borne by the Owner.

6. The Owner shall be solely responsible for all acts and behavior of the horse(s) at any time and hereby agrees to indemnify and hold the Operators harmless against all damages sustained or suffered by reason of the boarding of the horse(s) and for any claims or injuries whatsoever arising out of or in any way relating to the horse(s). Owner further agrees to pay any legal fees and/or expenses incurred by the Operators in defense of such claims.

7. Operators agree to attempt to contact Owner should Operators feel that medical treatment is needed for said horse(s) but, if Operators are unable to contact Owner, Operators are then authorized to secure emergency veterinary and/or blacksmith care required for the health and well being of said horse(s). All costs of such care secured shall be paid by the Owner within fifteen (15) days from the date Owner receives notice thereof, or Operators are authorized, as Owner's agent, to arrange direct billing to the Owner. The phone number to call for emergency situations is _____. The address for direct billing the Owner is _____

_____

_____.

8. Operators agree to provide the necessary shoeing and worming of the horse(s) as is reasonable and necessary. However, such expense for the same shall be the obligation of the Owner, upon presentation by Operators of the bill for such services rendered, including service charges, such bill shall be paid within fifteen (15) days from the date the bill is submitted to Owner.

9. Operators (shall/shall not) provide reasonable grooming for said horse(s) and the cost for this service (shall/shall not) become part of and included within the aforesaid fees. An additional fee of $_____ will be charged for this service.

10. The Owner represents and warrants to the Operators that it is the owner of the horse(s) free and clear of all liens and encumbrances whatsoever. The Owner agrees to notify the Operators of a sale of all or any interest in the horse(s) within seven (7) days after such event occurs. Notwithstanding a sale of all or any interest in the horse(s), the Owner shall remain fully bound by the terms of this Agreement unless otherwise indicated in a writing signed by both parties hereto. Prior to the time of delivery of said animal(s) to Operators, Owner shall provide proof satisfactory to Operators of negative Coggins tests for each horse.

11. Either party may terminate this Agreement for failure of the other party to meet any of the material terms of this agreement. In the case of any default by one party, the other party shall have the right to recover attorney's fees and court costs incurred as a result of said default.

12. This Agreement cannot be assigned by the Owner without the express written consent of the Operators.

13. Except as otherwise provided herein, the Agreement shall continue in full force and effect until terminated by either party by giving thirty (30) days written notice to the other party at the addresses specified within this Agreement.

14. The Operators shall have a lien on each horse for all unpaid boarding and other charges resulting from boarding of the horse(s) pursuant hereto, to include all costs for veterinary and blacksmith services which were advanced by Operators. The Owner agrees that in the event that the specified boarding charges plus late fees are not paid within thirty (30) days after they have become due and payable, in accordance with the terms hereof, the Operators may exercise their lien rights, and in connection therewith, may dispose of the horse(s) for any and all unpaid charges, at private or public sale, upon ten (10) days written notice. In the event such sale does not secure a sufficient price to pay the costs of board and other charges, plus the costs of the sale, the Owner shall immediately pay to the Operators sufficient funds to make up the difference. Any amounts realized by the Operators at such sale over and above the charges due and costs of such sale shall be retained by the Operators as liquidated damages for the breach of this Agreement by Owner. In addition, the Operators shall be entitled to notify any organization engaged in selling horses at public auction of the amount of unpaid boarding and other charges resulting from the boarding of the horse(s) and the Operators shall be entitled to receive from the proceeds of sale of the horse(s) all amounts due hereunder. The Operators shall have the right, without process of law, to retain the said horse(s) until the amount of all indebtedness is discharged.

15. All horses are required to be current of vaccinations as required by the Operators.

16. This Agreement shall be governed and construed in accordance with the laws of the State of _____.

17. This Agreement shall be binding upon and inure to the benefit of the parties hereto, and their heirs, personal representatives, successors and assigns.

IN WITNESS WHEREOF, the parties hereto have executed this Boarding Agreement as of the day, month and year first above written.

"OPERATORS"   "OWNER"

_____   _____

_____   _____

_____   _____
Address   Address

_____   _____
Telephone   Telephone

*Courtesy of Nicole Fox McCabe, Attorney at Law

HORSE TRANSPORTATION CONTRACT
Horse Shipping Company
22000 Nice Place Street
City, State 33355
800-555-0000

PICK-UP INFORMATION:

Name:_____

Address:_____

Phone:_____

Date of Pick-up:_____, 20___

DELIVERY INFORMATION:

Name:_____

Address:_____

Phone:_____

Date of Delivery:_____, 20___

HORSE INFORMATION:

Name:_____

Breed:_____ Registration Number:_____

Sex:_____ Age: _____ Color:_____

Identifying marks:_____

Name:_____

Breed:_____ Registration Number:_____

Sex:_____ Age: _____ Color:_____

Identifying marks:_____

Owner / Shipper (circle one) will provide hay and grain for horse while in shipment.

Feeding directions:_____
_____
_____

Special instructions:_____
_____
_____

PAYMENT INFORMATION:

Transportation cost: $_____

Supplies provided by Shipper: $_____

Total: $_____

Deposit (1/3 required): $_____

Balance due: $_____ on pick-up / delivery (circle one)

RELEASE:

The undersigned owner hereby releases and discharges Horse Shipping Company, here-inafter referred to as the Shipper, its agents or employees, from any and all liabilities, claims, demands or rights, which are related to or are in any way connected with the transport of the aforementioned horse(s) including but not limited to the negligent acts or omissions of the Shipper. The undersigned understands and acknowledges that $_____ mortality insurance per horse is provided by the Shipper. The undersigned agrees and covenants not to sue the Shipper for any injury, illness or damage to the aforementioned horse(s) and will hold the Shipper harmless for any liability that would incur for property damage or bodily injury to any horse(s), and/or persons loading, transporting, unloading or handling the aforementioned horse(s).

This constitutes the entire agreement between the horse owner and Shipper.

MY SIGNATURE BELOW INDICATES THAT I HAVE READ THIS ENTIRE AGREEMENT AND UNDERSTAND IT COMPLETELY. I hereby authorize the transportation of my horse(s) for the cost indicated. I understand that professional care will be taken to provide for the safety of my horse(s) and authorize veterinary care to be rendered at my expense should it be deemed necessary by the Shipper.

_____   _____
Owner's Signature   Date

Owner's Contact Information
Full Name:_____
Address:_____
Phone:_____

GUARANTEED LIVE FOAL BREEDING CONTRACT

THIS AGREEMENT, made and entered into this _____day of _____, 20_____, by and between _____, SELLER, the owner of a 20_____ season (the Season) to the thoroughbred stallion, _____, (the Stallion), and _____, PURCHASER.

1. PURCHASER agrees to breed the thoroughbred mare _____ to the Stallion during each normal cycle during the breeding season of 20_____ at _____Farm, located in _____. PURCHASER agrees to pay SELLER a total fee of $_____ plus _____% state sales tax payable as follows:

    PURCHASER agrees to pay $_____ payable on or before _____20____, unless said mare proves not in foal, in which case PURCHASER shall furnish a satisfactory veterinary certificate to that effect in lieu of payment. SELLER agrees that in the event said mare does not produce a live foal that can stand alone and nurse, SELLER shall refund the previously tendered fee to PURCHASER; provided , however, that PURCHASER must furnish a satisfactory veterinary certificate to SELLER and _____Farm stating that a live foal that can stand alone and nurse was not born as a result of this breeding. The veterinary certificate must be provided within fifteen (15) days of the date the mare fails to produce a live foal.

    In the event the mare provides twins, SELLER further agrees to refund to PURCHASER the previously tendered fee upon certification that neither foal shall be registered as a thoroughbred. This certificate must be provided SELLER and _____Farm within fifteen (15) days of the date said mare foals.

    In the event PURCHASER defaults in payment of any sums due SELLER, and such default continues for a period of ninety (90) days, this agreement becomes a no guarantee of live foal agreement and no refund shall be due PURCHASER for any reason. In the event PURCHASER fails to provide any certificate required by this agreement with such default continuing for a period of fifteen (15) days, this agreement becomes a no guarantee live foal and no refund shall be due hereunder for any reason.

2. PAYMENTS, REFUNDS, NOTICE AND INQUIRIES UNDER THIS CONTRACT MUST BE MADE TO:

    _____
    _____
    _____

3. PURCHASER further agrees that said mare is registered as a thoroughbred and shall be healthy, free from disease or infection that could be transmitted to the Stallion and in sound breeding condition. The PURCHASER'S presentation of the mare is his representation that the mare is healthy and sound for breeding; however, if requested, PURCHASER shall furnish a satisfactory veterinary certificate to that effect.

   It is understood and agreed that the Farm Management reserves the right to refuse to permit the breeding of any mare to the Stallion if and when, in the opinion of the veterinarian attending the Stallion, such breeding would be detrimental to the health and welfare of the Stallion.

4. This contract is personal to the PURCHASER and shall not be assigned or transferred by the PURCHASER without the prior written permission of the SELLER.

5. In the event the mare is sold, catalogued and transferred to a sales facility, transported out of the continental United States, or changes ownership, the fee, if unpaid, shall immediately become due and payable and there shall be no refund of said fee to anyone under any circumstances, and specifically, any live foal guarantee previously made in paragraph 1 shall be deemed to be waived by PURCHASER and his/her successors and assigns.

6. It is further agreed that neither SELLER nor PURCHASER shall be liable for or responsible to either party for any disease, accident, injury or death to said mare or the Stallion. In case of a contagious disease on the farm where the mare is boarded, the mare may not be accepted for breeding. In the event the mare is rejected, no damages shall be due to PURCHASER.

7. Should the mare die or become unfit for breeding prior to being covered for the first time by the Stallion, PURCHASER has the right to substitute a mare, providing the substitute mare is approved by the SELLER and Farm Manager and the SELLER is notified within seven (7) business days of the death or injury of the original mare named in this contract. Such notice must be in writing and received in the offices of _____ at the address set forth in paragraph 2 above. Such written notice must be accompanied by a veterinarian certificate attesting to the death or the nature of the injury or disease or breeding unsoundness of the mare.

8. Should the mare die or become unfit for breeding for any reason after she has been covered by the Stallion, PURCHASER shall have no right to substitute a mare.

9. If the original approved mare or the substitute approved mare is not bred, then all sums set out in paragraph number 1 are due and owing SELLER. In the event PURCHASER does not present a mare to the Stallion for reasons other than cited herein, PURCHASER shall be liable for total fees set out in numbered paragraph

1 above. If either mare is bred to any other Stallion in the same breeding season without the SELLER'S permission, PURCHASER agrees to pay to SELLER within ten (10) days the stud fee hereinabove set out in paragraph 1 without regard to any other terms, conditions or waivers herein set forth. PURCHASER acknowledges that SELLER has reserved a breeding nomination to the Stallion for the sole use of PURCHASER'S mare.

10. In order to secure payment of the breeding fee provided for hereinabove, PUR-CHASER grant to SELLER and _____Farm as agent for SELLER, a security interest in the foal to be produced and appoints _____Farm as PURCHASER'S attorney-in-fact for the purpose of executing financing statements. PURCHASER further grants to SELLER and _____Farm, agent for SELLER, a security interest in the Stallion Service Certificate applicable to the foal produced as a result of the breeding season sold herein, and a security interest in any other stallion service certificates in the possession of _____Farm in which PURCHASER may have an interest.

11. The within contract shall be null, void and of no effect unless it is signed by PUR-CHASER and returned to _____ within fourteen (14) days of the date set out hereinabove. This contract shall become null, void and of no effect unless PURCHASER shall designate in writing the name of the mare and the name and address of the farm where the mare is kept, with said notice to be received in the offices of _____ prior to February 1 immediately preceding the breeding season, or within fourteen (14) days of signing this contract, whichever date is later.

12. PURCHASER and SELLER agree that should the Stallion die or be sold by its owners or, for whatever reason, become unfit for service before first servicing the mare, or for two consecutive heat cycles, this contract shall be null and void.

13. This Agreement shall be binding upon the parties hereto, their heirs, personal representatives, successors and assigns and shall be construed and governed in accordance with the laws of the State of _____. Jurisdiction and venue for any action arising as a result of this contract shall be in_____ County, _____. In the case of any default by one party, the party not in default shall have the right to recover attorney's fees and court costs suffered as a result of enforcing his/her rights under this contract.

14. The parties hereto further acknowledge that the within contract contains the entire agreement of the parties and that neither of the parties hereto is relying upon any verbal assurances of whatever nature that are not contained and expressed in this contract. This contract may not be modified, changed or amended except by a writing signed by the parties. It is further agreed and understood that PURCHASER will be bound by and comply with the terms and conditions of any syndication agreement to which the rights of the shareholder in the Stallion are subject.

15. If the season sold under this Contract is owned in partnership, the person signing this Contract is authorized to act on behalf of the partnership and, if necessary, is responsible for refunding the stud fee in full. If the season sold under this contract is owned by a corporation, the person signing this Contract is authorized to act on behalf of said corporation and, if necessary, is personally responsible for refunding the stud fee in full. If the mare bred under this contract is owned in partnership, the person signing this Contract is authorized to act on behalf of the partnership and the person signing this Contract is personally responsible for paying the stud fee in full. If the mare bred under this contract is owned by a corporation, the person signing this Contract is authorized to act on behalf of the corporation and the person signing this Contract is personally responsible for paying the stud fee in full.

16. SELLER warrants the ownership of this breeding nomination and that it is free and clear of all liens and/or encumbrances and that it has the right to sell this breeding nomination and needs no consent from the _____ or any other person or entity to confirm this sale. SELLER warrants that upon full payment of all sums due under this Contract, he/she has the right to issue PURCHASER the Stallion Service Certificate. SELLER further warrants that upon full payment of all sums due under this Contract, it will promptly issue or cause to be issued said Stallion Service Certificate.

17. PURCHASER agrees to abide by the rules and shed requirements as set forth by _____ Farm for the breeding season.

18. In the event the fees set out hereinabove or any portion thereof, shall not be paid when due, then to the extent permitted by law, PURCHASER agrees to pay interest and service charges of one and one-half percent (1½%) per month, commencing thirty (30) days after any sum is due hereunder.

IN WITNESS WHEREOF, the parties hereto have executed multiple copies of this contract, each copy to have the force and effect of an original, on the day and year first above written.

_____   _____
SELLER   PURCHASER

_____   _____
ADDRESS   ADDRESS

_____   _____

_____   _____
DATE   DATE

*Courtesy of Nicole Fox McCabe, Attorney at Law

SHIPPED SEMEN BREEDING AGREEMENT

THIS AGREEMENT made and entered into this _____ day of _____, 20___, by and between, _____, ("Seller") and _____, ("Purchaser")

RECITALS:

    A. Seller owns the stallion _____, a registered _____ foaled _____.

    B. Purchaser owns the mare _____ and desires to breed said mare to Seller's stallion.

NOW, THEREFORE, for good and valuable consideration, the parties hereby agree as follows:

1. The stud fee shall be _____ ($_____) and shall become due and payable thirty (30) days before the expected breeding date.

2. The shipping fee of _____ ($_____) per shipment includes costs associated with shipping of Equitainer® to Purchaser or Purchaser's designated Veterinarian and the subsequent return of Equitainer® to Seller. The shipping fee shall become due and payable thirty (30) days before the expected breeding date.

3. Purchaser agrees to pay Seller a booking fee of _____($_____) on the booking date. Booking will be limited.

4. A deposit of _____ ($_____) will be required for the Equitainer®. Seller agrees to refund total amount of said deposit to Purchaser within seven business days of the return of Equitainer® to Seller. A prepaid return shipment form for overnight delivery will be enclosed with the Equitainer®.

   The remainder of the stud fees, the shipping fee, and the refundable deposit for the Equitainer® (see below) will be due 30 days prior to expected breeding date.

5. Purchaser agrees to have a uterine culture performed by a licensed veterinarian before semen is requested. A copy of the veterinarian's certificate must be received by Seller prior to shipping the semen.

6. Purchaser agrees to give vaccinations of Pneumabort-K to said mare when pregnant as recommended by their veterinarian.

7. Seller guarantees to ship live semen with a concentration level adequate to inseminate one mare. In the event that Purchaser's mare does not take and become in foal, Seller agrees to breed said mare again for no additional stud fee during the current breeding season and the breeding season immediately following, provided said mare has been examined by a veterinarian. Purchaser shall be responsible for any shipping fees and Equitainer® deposits.

8. Seller offers purchaser a live foal guarantee. A live foal is able to stand and nurse for at least forty-eight (48) hours after birth. In the event that said mare does not deliver a live foal, Purchaser shall notify the Seller within seven (7) business days and provide the Seller with a written Veterinary Statement which will include the physical condition of the mare upon examination, examination of the foal and the reason for death of the foal. Seller agrees to give Purchaser the right to an additional service to said mare (or substitute mare), at any time within eighteen (18) months from the last date of breeding said mare under this Agreement. Seller shall have no further liability hereunder for servicing said mare.

7. Seller agrees to execute all necessary documents for the registration of the offspring of the breeding. Seller will not be responsible for registration or registration fees of the foal.

8. Either party may terminate this Agreement for failure of other party to meet any material terms of this Agreement. In the case of any default by one party, the wronged party shall have the right to recover reasonable attorney's fees and court costs as a result of said default. In the event that the stallion dies, or in any way becomes unfit for breeding, then this Agreement becomes null and void and any deposit will be returned to Purchaser.

9. Purchaser cannot assign this Agreement without the express written consent of Seller.

10. This Agreement shall be binding upon the parties hereto, their heirs, personal representatives, successors and assigns and shall be construed and governed in accordance with the laws of the State of _____. Jurisdiction and venue for any action arising as a result of this contract shall be in _____County, _____.

11. The parties hereto further acknowledge that the within contract contains the entire agreement of the parties and that neither of the parties hereto is relying upon any verbal assurances of whatever nature that are not contained and expressed in this contract.

WITNESS the following signatures and seals:

Seller:_____ Date: _____

Purchaser:_____ Date: _____

Purchaser Information:

Print Name:_____

Address_____

City _____ State: _____ Zip Code_____

Phone _____

Mare's Registered Name and Number _____

Purchaser's Veterinarian and contact information:_____
_____
_____

AFTERWORD

Just as a strategic business plan must change and evolve with market trends and current events, so must your personal financial plan. Good financial decisions—those that are made with the long-term in mind--require sufficient knowledge and an ability to view options from different angles. I urge everyone to consult financial, legal, and accounting professionals and seek experts in other areas as well.

Remember, when personal matters are the focus, ask yourself two questions: "Does my decision benefit me and/or my family?" and "Does my decision make good sense financially?" And, when you must make a decision related to your horse or horses, throw in a third question, "Does this benefit my horse?"

Don't forget to enjoy today. Go to that horseshow. If your budget allows, buy that mare you really want. Owning horses makes every day more enjoyable, and having such a passion in life makes those long work meetings a little more bearable. As my father always says, "Wealth is nice, but you can't take it with you."

So, live your life to the fullest, fund your retirement, and invest wisely.

APPENDIX I

Net Worth Worksheet

1. What are your assets?

Cash in savings and checking	$_____
Certificates of deposits	$_____
Money-market funds	$_____
Mutual funds	$_____
Stocks	$_____
Bonds	$_____
Real estate investment funds	$_____
401(K) or 403(b) plans	$_____
Individual retirement accounts	$_____
Vested equity in pensions	$_____
Vested equity in profit sharing	$_____
Keogh plans	$_____
Life insurance (cash value)	$_____
Annuities (surrender value)	$_____
Market value of home	$_____
Market value of other real estate	$_____
Other investments	$_____
Household furnishings (low estimate)	$_____
Automobiles	$_____
Boats, horse trailers	$_____
Furs, jewelry, fine arts	$_____
Horses	$_____
Other assets	$_____
Total assets	**$_____**

2. What are your liabilities?

Mortgages	$_____
Automobile loans	$_____
Student loans	$_____
Home equity loans	$_____
Home equity credit lines	$_____
Personal credit lines	$_____
Credit card (1)	$_____
Credit card (2)	$_____
Credit card (3)	$_____
Credit card (4)	$_____
Credit card (5)	$_____
Other debt	$_____
Total liabilities	**$_____**

3. Subtract liabilities from assets:

Total assets	$_____
Total liabilities	$_____
Net worth	**$_____**

Monthly Budget Worksheet

Total assets $_____
Budget for the month of _____, 20_____

Item	*	Budgeted	Actual	Difference
Automobile maintenance	——	$_____	$_____	$_____
New tires	——	$_____	$_____	$_____
Automobile insurance	——	$_____	$_____	$_____
Automobile loans	——	$_____	$_____	$_____
Homeowner's insurance	——	$_____	$_____	$_____
Horse owner's insurance	——	$_____	$_____	$_____
Christmas and birthday gifts	——	$_____	$_____	$_____
Taxes not withheld	——	$_____	$_____	$_____
Mortgage	——	$_____	$_____	$_____
Groceries/household items	——	$_____	$_____	$_____
Gas	——	$_____	$_____	$_____
Electricity	——	$_____	$_____	$_____
Telephone	——	$_____	$_____	$_____
Cell phone	——	$_____	$_____	$_____
Clothing/dry cleaning	——	$_____	$_____	$_____
Personal care	——	$_____	$_____	$_____
Vacation	——	$_____	$_____	$_____
Farrier	——	$_____	$_____	$_____
Veterinarian	——	$_____	$_____	$_____
Medications (animal)	——	$_____	$_____	$_____
Wormer, flyspray, ointments	——	$_____	$_____	$_____
Hay	——	$_____	$_____	$_____
Grain and supplies	——	$_____	$_____	$_____
Bedding	——	$_____	$_____	$_____
Riding instruction	——	$_____	$_____	$_____
Pasture management	——	$_____	$_____	$_____
Savings/investment	——	$_____	$_____	$_____
_____	——	$_____	$_____	$_____
_____	——	$_____	$_____	$_____
_____	——	$_____	$_____	$_____
_____	——	$_____	$_____	$_____
_____	——	$_____	$_____	$_____

* Denotes amounts set aside for future payments on item

Cash Requirement Worksheet

Cash requirement worksheet as of _____, 20_____

Item					
Amount	$_____	$_____	$_____	$_____	$_____
Due date					
Save	$_____/Mo.	$_____/Mo.	$_____/Mo.	$_____/Mo.	$_____/Mo.
Bal. forward	$_____	$_____	$_____	$_____	$_____
Jan	$_____	$_____	$_____	$_____	$_____
Feb	$_____	$_____	$_____	$_____	$_____
March	$_____	$_____	$_____	$_____	$_____
April	$_____	$_____	$_____	$_____	$_____
May	$_____	$_____	$_____	$_____	$_____
June	$_____	$_____	$_____	$_____	$_____
July	$_____	$_____	$_____	$_____	$_____
Aug	$_____	$_____	$_____	$_____	$_____
Sept	$_____	$_____	$_____	$_____	$_____
Oct	$_____	$_____	$_____	$_____	$_____
Nov	$_____	$_____	$_____	$_____	$_____
Dec	$_____	$_____	$_____	$_____	$_____
Total left for item:	$_____	$_____	$_____	$_____	$_____

Total in the bill paying account: $_____

APPENDIX II

Glossary

This glossary is divided into three main sections: *Accounting, Legal and Real Estate*; *Investments*; **and** *Insurance*. **The definitions and terms herein include those from the Virginia State Corporation Commission's Bureau of Insurance, the Commission's Division of Securities, and the United States Department of Housing and Urban Development.**

ACCOUNTING, LEGAL AND REAL ESTATE

Amendment: A proposed alteration concerning a written document acknowledged by all involved parties.

Appraisal: The fair market value of property determined by an authorized person and by comparing sales of similar property on the open market.

Asset: One's property, whether real or personal, tangible or intangible, that can be assigned a monetary value.

Assignment: The transfer of responsibilities under an agreement to another party.

Balance sheet: The listing of one's assets, liabilities, and equity as of a specified date. Assets should be equal to liabilities plus equity in double entry accounting.

Capacity: The mental competence and legal age to enter into a contract.

Contingency: A condition of sale specified in a purchase contract.

Contract: A legal, enforceable agreement. A contract must have the following four elements: mutual assent, consideration, capacity, and legality.

Contractor: One who agrees to perform specified work for a stated fee and is not an employee.

Consideration: Monetary inducement for a party to enter into a contract.

Cost versus benefit analysis (cost-benefit analysis): The conceptual framework for decision-making wherein resources should only be spent if the expected benefits (returns) from the expenditure are greater than the actual costs of the expenditure.

Deed: The document that transfers title to real property.

Deposit (earnest money): A sum of money provided by a buyer to illustrate the intent to complete the contracted transaction (i.e., purchase the piece of property).

Direct-costing (variable-costing): A system used for budgeting, decision-making, and cost control wherein costs are classified as either *fixed* (those that remain constant whether one or multiple items are produced) or *variable* (those that increase with the number of items produced: higher production, higher costs.)

Equity: The money value of property without any liens or obligations against it.

Liability: An accounting debt of an amount that can be measured or a legal obligation or responsibility.

Lien: A claim laid by one person or company on the property of another as security for money owed.

Liquidity: Having the cash flow available to pay all debts and obligations as they become due.

Loan: Money furnished to a borrower for temporary use with the understanding it be returned with interest.

Lock-in: A lender's written commitment that the interest rate or points offered at the time of loan application, or during the processing of a loan, will remain the same until settlement or closing of the escrow process.

Mechanic's liens: Claims for payment by contractors and material suppliers against newly constructed buildings and other improvements to a property.

Mortgage broker: A company that buys mortgages from lenders, and then sells them to buyers.

Mortgage clause: The clause in a real estate contract that ensures your deposit will be refunded if the sale is canceled because you are unable to get a mortgage loan.

Mortgage insurance: Private and government mortgage insurance protect the lender against default, enabling the lender to make a loan considered to be a higher risk. Lenders often require mortgage insurance for loans where the down payment is less than 20 percent of the sale price.

Mutual assent: The parties to contract have a "meeting of minds" and agree to the promises and terms of the contract.

Net worth (owner's equity): The value of a business or person that is free from encumbrances. (Assets minus liabilities equals net worth.)

Personal property: Generally, all tangible property *except* for real property.

Point: A fee that equals 1 percent of a loan amount. Points are usually paid to the lender, mortgage broker, or both at the settlement or upon the completion of the escrow. Often, you can pay fewer points in exchange for a higher interest rate or more points for a lower rate.

Probate: The court's recognition of a will as valid and enforceable.

Probate estate: The property that is handled or distributed by an executor or administrator of a will.

Promises made: The warranties and representations made to the other party by each party to a contract.

Real property: Real estate, including land, buildings, and fixtures.

Settlement agent/escrow agent: The party that handles all of the details of a real estate closing and holds funds in escrow for both buyer and seller.

Settlement costs: The costs associated with the transfer of legal title to real estate, including taxes and title insurance, among other things. You can negotiate which settlement costs are the responsibility of the buyer, and which are the responsibility of the seller.

Severability: The ability to extract or remove one part or provision in a contract without altering the enforceability of the rest of the contract.

Survey: A drawing of a property showing the perimeter boundaries and marking the location of the house and other improvements.

Tangible assets: Assets that have shape and form. Real estate, horses, cars, and clothing are examples of tangible assets.

Time value of money: One of the fundamental concepts in financial management. A dollar received today is worth more than a dollar received at some point in the future, because you can invest and earn interest on today's dollar.

Title: The legal ownership of property.

Title search: The process of reviewing all recorded transactions having to do with a particular piece of property to determine if a title defect exists that could interfere with a transfer of ownership.

Trusts: Separate legal entities that can hold and invest property. Trusts are typically *inter vivos* (living trusts) or testamentary (created through a will).

Truth in lending disclosure statement: A document that shows the annual percentage rate (APR) and other payment information for a loan.

Waiver: To release or give up a claim or right.

Will: A legally enforceable document that declares how an individual wishes his or her probate property to be distributed.

Zoning: Regulations that control the use of land within a jurisdiction.

INVESTMENT

Aggressive growth (speculation): A risky investment approach intended to achieve high profits, generally focused on companies in developing or unstable industries.

Annuities: Contracts that provide for a specified income payable to an insured, at regular intervals over a certain period of time.

Back-end loads: Deferred sales charges that may decline over time, and may have to be paid when an investor sells his or her mutual fund shares.

Broker-dealer: Any firm that participates in the offer and sale of securities.

Cash account: The commonly used account with a broker-dealer that requires that transactions are paid in full.

Certificates of deposit (CDs): Negotiable securities issued by commercial banks against money deposited for them. They are guaranteed by the FDIC, subject to limitations.

Common stock: Represents a voting ownership interest in a corporation.

Convertible securities: Securities bought with an investor's right (usually conditional) to convert the securities to another form. For example, common stock purchased with rights to convert it to preferred stock at a later date.

Derivatives: Contractual relationships established by two or more parties where payment is based on or derived from some specific, or multiple standard(s). Common derivative products are futures, options, forward contracts, stripped mortgage-backed securities, and structured notes.

Discount broker-dealers: Dealers who execute trades, but do not conduct any market research for the investor's benefit, make recommendations, or provide investment advice.

Discretionary account: Complete discretionary authority allows your agent or representative to decide, without consulting you, which securities to purchase or sell, when to do so, and how much to pay or accept for them.

Front-end loads: Commissions paid to the broker-dealer and agent when an investor buys mutual funds.

Full service broker-dealer: Firm that provides a range of services, such as conducting market research, offering advice on which investment products to purchase, offering financial, estate, and tax planning services, as well as managed accounts.

Growth funds: Tend to invest in companies experiencing rapidly expanding revenues and profits, the majority of which are reinvested to fuel further growth.

Income funds: A fairly conservative investment approach designed for immediate income as interest or dividends.

Investment advisor: Any firm that provides the public with investment advice related to purchasing securities for compensation.

Investment advisor service: Generally offer more than just advice on which securities to buy. Types of services vary widely, including financial analysis, financial model development (for use as an investment strategy), and recommendations on broker-dealer services.

Management fees: Fees charged to investors to cover the management expenses of a mutual fund.

Margin account: Allows you to buy securities by borrowing money from the broker-dealer. Buying securities "on margin" can mean greater profits, but only if earnings exceed the margin borrowing expenses.

Money market funds: Mutual funds that invest in short-term debt instruments, such as US government securities, bank CDs, and other types of commercial paper. They are appropriate for investors who want immediate income, low risk, and easy access to their funds.

Municipal securities: Negotiable debt obligations issued by towns, cities, counties, or other subdivisions of a state or municipality, which are backed by the good faith and/or taxing power of the municipality. They are usually appropriate for investors seeking predictable income and moderate safety.

Mutual funds: Investment companies that purchase stocks, bonds, and other assets by combining the dollars from a pool of individuals and institutions who share common financial goals.

Preferred stock: Represents a non-voting ownership interest in a corporation. Preferred shareholders usually receive fixed dividends that are senior to, and payable before, any common stock dividends and they may also have preference in the distribution of assets.

Real estate investment trusts (REITs): Trusts that invest in real estate properties or mortgages, generally suitable for investors seeking capital appreciation and income.

Safety: A conservative investment approach with only modest risk and only a modest expected profit.

Tolerance level: An investor's ability to accept the worst case investment scenario—a loss. The ability to sustain a loss depends on wealth and investment strategy.

US government securities: Negotiable debt obligations of various government agencies, guaranteed or backed by the full faith and credit of the United States government.

Wrap fees: Single charges for packages of services, such as combined brokerage and investment advisory services. Unlike commission-based fees, wrap fees normally are not related to the number, size, or frequency of transactions.

INSURANCE

(This section is divided into three subsections.)

General and Medical Insurance for Equines and Humans

Balance billing: When a health care plan allows a provider (doctor or hospital) to bill the insured (member) for the portion of the total medical charges that his or her plan does not cover.

Coinsurance: The percentage of health care allowable charges you must pay after you have met your deductible.

Coordination of benefits (COB): Method of integrating benefits payable under more than one health insurance plan so the insured's benefits from all sources do not exceed 100 percent of allowable medical expenses.

Co-payment: A specific charge the insured must pay for a medical service. For example, you may be responsible for $10 of the cost of a medical appointment and the health plan covers the remaining charges.

Cost sharing: Policy provisions that require an individual to pay—via co-payments, deductibles, and coinsurance—a portion of his or her health care expenses.

Deductible: The amount of medical care expenses you are responsible for, generally annually, before your insurance policy or HMO plan takes effect.

Elimination period: A specified number of days at the beginning of each period of disability or hospital confinement during which no benefits are paid.

Evidence of coverage (EOC): Document that summarizes the provisions and benefits of a managed care health insurance plan.

Evidence of insurability: A statement or proof of physical condition and/or other information affecting a person's eligibility for insurance.

Exclusions: Specific conditions or circumstances for which a policy or plan will not provide benefits.

Explanation of benefits (EOB): The statement sent to a participant in a health policy or managed care plan listing services, amounts paid by the plan, and total amount billed to the patient.

Fee-for-service: A health care payment system where the provider is paid for each service rendered rather than a pre-negotiated amount per patient.

Formulary: List of prescription medications covered by an insurance company.

Grace period: Specified time (usually 31 days) following the premium due date during which insurance remains in force and a policyholder may pay the premium without penalty.

Guaranteed renewable contract: Contract under which an insured has the right (commonly up to a certain age) to continue the policy by the timely payment of premiums.

Health maintenance organization (HMO): A prepaid, managed care health insurance plan in which the insured pays a premium and the HMO then covers the cost of visits to doctors, hospitals, and other providers within the HMO's network.

Indemnity plan: Traditional health insurance that covers a percentage of the cost of care (often 80 percent) after the consumer pays an annual deductible. Patients with an indemnity plan can choose any doctor or hospital for their care.

Lifetime maximum: The total amount of benefits that a health care plan will pay over a policyholder's lifetime.

Loss of use: Coverage for equines that is similar to disability insurance for people. If a horse can no longer perform his "job," such as race or jump, the insurance will compensate the owner for the loss of value.

Managed care health insurance plan (MCHIP): A type of health care plan that can limit coverage to those hospitals or physicians ("network providers") that work for or contract with them. (See also "Health maintenance organization.")

Maximum out-of-pocket costs: The most a member will pay when considering co-payments, coinsurance, deductibles, etc., usually on a calendar year or policy year basis.

Medicaid: A joint state and federal public assistance program that pays for health care services for low income or disabled persons.

Medicare: A federally administered health insurance program that covers the cost of hospitalization, medical care, and some related services for people over the age of 65, those receiving Social Security Disability Insurance payments, and those with End Stage Renal Disease (ESRD).

Medicare supplement insurance (Medigap policy): Insurance coverage sold on an individual or group basis, which helps to fill the gaps in the protection provided by the Medicare program.

Multiple employer welfare arrangement (MEWA): An arrangement by which two or more employers form a coalition to offer a health plan to their employees.

Non-cancelable: A health insurance policy that the insured has a right to continue in force by payment of premiums for a period of time, as set forth in the contract.

Out-of-network care: Medical services obtained by managed care health insurance plan members from non-participating or non-preferred providers (i.e., doctors and hospitals).

Out-of-pocket costs: Health care costs the insured must pay out of his or her own pocket, including coinsurance, co-payments, deductibles, etc.

Preadmission (or precertification) authorization: A requirement that the health care plan must approve, in advance, certain hospital admissions or certain procedures.

Preexisting condition exclusion: A limitation or exclusion of health benefits based on the fact that a physical or mental condition was present before the first day of coverage.

Preferred provider organization (PPO): A network of health care providers that have agreed to provide medical services to a health plan's members at discounted costs. The cost to use physicians within the PPO network is generally less than using out-of-network providers.

Premium: The amount you pay in exchange for insurance coverage.

Primary care physician (PCP): The physician, internist, or pediatrician who manages your healthcare under most HMOs/MCHIPs. A PCP makes referrals to specialists if necessary.

Rescind: To nullify or make void a policy or coverage.

Life Insurance

Accidental death benefit: Sometimes known as "double" or "triple indemnity," this rider increases the death benefit paid if the insured dies as a result of a covered accident.

Automatic premium loan: An optional provision that requires an insurance company to collect any past due premium by means of a policy loan, therefore preventing the policy from lapsing (provided the available loan value is sufficient to pay the premium).

Beneficiary: Person named by the policyowner to receive the policy benefits at the death of the insured.

Cash value: The amount an insurance company will pay the policyowner if a permanent whole life insurance policy is surrendered or otherwise terminated.

Contingent beneficiary: Person named by the policyowner to receive the proceeds of the policy should the primary or first beneficiary die before the insured.

Convertibility (conversion privilege): Some term life policies can be switched (converted) to a permanent whole life policy without proof of insurability.

Dependent children rider: Generally provides level term coverage for dependent children up to a stated age.

Disability income rider: Provides a monthly income if the policyholder becomes disabled.

Face value (face amount): The initial amount of death benefit provided by a policy. The actual death benefit may be higher or lower depending on the options selected, outstanding policy loans, or premium owed.

Grace period: After the first premium payment, life insurance policies provide a minimum grace period of 31 days after the due date to make the next premium payment. If the premium is not paid before the grace period expires, the policy will lapse.

Group life insurance: Provides coverage for a group of people under one "master" contract.

Guaranteed insurability: Guarantees the insured the right to purchase additional life insurance on specified dates, with rates based on the attained age of the insured.

Guaranteed renewable: A policy provision wherein the insurance company must renew coverage at the insured's request when the term period ends.

Incontestability: Generally, after a policy has been in force for two years, the insurance company cannot contest the validity of the policy for any reason other than nonpayment of premium.

Lapse: Termination of a policy because of failure to pay the premium.

Level term rider: Provides extra term insurance protection for a specific amount of time.

Long term care rider: Pays benefits if the insured meets defined policy eligibility criteria (if he or she is confined to a long term care facility, for example). The maximum benefit is generally a percentage of the life insurance policy's face amount. Usually, the death benefit will be reduced by the amount paid out under this rider.

Mortgage protection: Provides an additional term life insurance benefit to ensure the policyowner's ability to make mortgage payments.

Nonforfeiture benefits: Provisions that may be available in the event a policy lapses due to nonpayment of premium, such as reduced paid-up insurance (the policy's cash value is used to buy paid-up life insurance of the same plan type as the original policy but in a lower amount than the original face value); extended term (the available cash value of the policy is used to purchase term insurance); and cash surrender (allows the owner to receive a policy's available cash value in a lump sum).

Participating versus non-participating: Participating policies may pay dividends (refunds of any excess or unused premiums), while non-participating policies do not.

Policy loans: A policyholder may borrow an amount up to the maximum loan value of a whole life policy.

Reinstatement: The restoration of a lapsed policy to its original premium-paying status. The company may require evidence of insurability and all past due premiums, plus interest.

Surrender: Voluntary cancellation of a policy for its cash value.

Term life: Life insurance that offers protection for a set period of time (the policy term) and pays a death benefit only if you die during that term. Generally, this type of insurance offers the largest amount of pure insurance protection for the lowest premium. There are three major types of term life insurance: level term (the death benefit stays the same and premiums remain constant throughout the policy term); increasing term (the benefit—and the premium too—increases by specific amounts and at intervals as specified in the policy); and decreasing term (the benefit decreases periodically as specified by the policy; however, premiums remain constant).

Underwriter: The person who reviews applications for insurance and decides if the applicant is an acceptable risk to the company.

Universal life: A type of permanent insurance where the premiums paid, less expense charges, are deposited into an interest-earning policy account. Charges for the insurance are deducted from the account, and coverage continues as long as there is enough money in the account to pay the related charges.

Variable life: A type of permanent life insurance where the death benefit and cash value depend upon the performance of investments—such as stocks and bonds—underlying the policy. These policies are so investment-dependent they can only be sold by an agent registered as a securities dealer.

Waiver of premium: In the event the insured becomes disabled, as defined in a policy, the insurance company pays the premium during the disability period.

Whole life (straight life, ordinary life): A type of permanent life insurance that protects you for as long as you live and the premiums are paid. Generally maintains the same premium for the duration of the insured's life or a set amount of time. This type of policy accumulates cash value.

Property & Casualty Insurance

Actual cash value (ACV): The value of property figured by first determining what it would cost to replace the property (see "Replacement cost") and then adjusting that figure by subtracting an amount that reflects depreciation.

Additional living expense: Covers temporary expenses for hotel/apartment living while the insured is unable to live in his or her home because of damage caused by a peril covered by his or her homeowner's policy.

Automobile liability: A person's responsibility to others for bodily injury or property damage caused by his or her automobile.

Boiler and machinery: Insurance that provides protection for damages caused by equipment that keeps a business in operation, basically insuring against the three major exclusions found in most property insurance policies: (1) boiler explosion; (2) mechanical breakdown; and (3) electrical arcing.

Builders' risk coverage: Covers buildings during the course of construction either for the full value of the finished building or on the value of the building at the time of loss.

Building ordinance coverage: Insurance companies are required to offer the option of buying coverage that pays the cost of repairing or replacing property in accordance with local building codes.

Business interruption insurance: Covers a business's loss of earnings due to damage to or destruction of property. This coverage generally provides reimbursement for salaries, taxes, rents, and other expenses plus net profits that would have been earned during the period of interruption.

Coinsurance: Reflects the minimum amount of insurance a policyholder must carry before the insurance company will fully reimburse him or her for a loss.

Collision coverage: Insurance coverage for your automobile when it overturns or collides with another car or object.

Commercial crime coverage: Purchased by a business to cover stock and fixtures in the event of burglary and robbery, protect money and securities, or protect against counterfeit currency or employee dishonesty.

Commercial general liability (CGL): Provides many business liability coverages under one contract, including premises and operations coverage (pays bodily injury and property damage claims to members of the public as a result of an accident on business premises or arising out of business operations) and products and completed operations coverage (covers liability arising from the handling, use of, existence of any condition in, or warranty of any goods or products manufactured, sold, handled or distributed by your business after the product is given to others and is away from the business premises).

Comprehensive coverage: Coverage for losses to an automobile, such as fire, vandalism, water, hail, glass breakage, wind, falling objects, and vehicle theft (but not collision).

Deductible: The amount the insured must pay before benefits from the insurance company are payable. The higher the deductible, the lower the premium.

Directors' and officers' liability insurance: Protects corporate officers and directors against claims brought by shareholders, employees, consumers, clients, or businesses because of wrongful acts committed in the course of their executive duties.

Errors and omissions insurance: Coverage available for individuals, such as corporate directors and officers, who may be held liable for losses caused by their errors or oversights.

Fidelity bonds: Cover business owners for losses due to dishonest acts by their employees. Bonds can be purchased to cover specific individuals or positions, or "blanket bonds" can be written to cover all employees of the organization.

Inland marine insurance: Coverage that is written primarily to cover property in transit (i.e., from warehouse to warehouse) as well as property in the custody of bailees, such as dry cleaners, processors, laundries, etc. May also be used to cover sales samples, contractors' equipment, patterns, exhibitions, and live animals, including horses and cattle.

Liability coverage: Coverage for injury to another person or another person's belongings when the loss is the insured's fault.

Loss of income benefit: In the event of an accident, coverage is provided for the insured or others in the insured's automobile for income loss up to $100 per week, not exceeding 52 weeks.

Medical expense: Covers the medical or funeral expenses of a person who is injured or killed in an automobile accident. The coverage applies no matter who is at fault.

Medical payments coverage: Covers medical expenses for a person who is injured in an accident at the insured's home regardless of fault (does not include coverage for the insured or a member of the insured's household).

Named peril policy: Covers any loss that is caused by one of the covered perils named (specified) in the policy.

Open perils policy: Covers damage or loss from all causes, except causes that are specifically excluded.

Out-building (other structures or appurtenant structures): Covers detached buildings on an insured's property, such as a tool shed or garage.

Owners' and contractors' protective liability: Provides liability coverage for an insured who is sued because of the negligent acts or omissions of an independent contractor or subcontractor hired by the insured, which result in bodily injury or property damage to a third party.

Peril: Cause or event that causes a loss, such as fire, lightning, or theft.

Personal property or contents: Includes everything in the insured's home such as clothes, furniture, and appliances.

Professional liability insurance: Coverage that pays liability claims arising from wrongful acts, errors and omissions, and malpractice by physicians, attorneys, or other professionals.

Property damage coverage: Coverage for the insured's house and personal property.

Rental reimbursement: Provides temporary coverage for the rental of a substitute vehicle while the insured's cannot be driven because of a collision or comprehensive loss.

Replacement cost: The replacement cost of a building equals the amount it would cost to construct the house or building today using materials of the same kind and quality.

Surety bonds: A financial guarantee of the performance of a specific action. For example, a builder may be required by his client to buy a bond under the terms of a construction contract. If the builder fails to perform as agreed, the client can get a settlement. The bonding company will then seek reimbursement from the builder who is the principal under the surety bond.

Umbrella liability insurance: Provides protection over and above the limits of basic liability policies, such as commercial general liability policies and commercial automobile policies.

Uninsured/underinsured motorist coverage: Coverage that applies when the insured is injured in an auto accident caused by a person who does not have insurance, a driver whose liability limits are not high enough to cover your damages, or a hit-and-run driver.

Workers compensation insurance: Offers coverage to an employee if injured on the job; for most employers, it is required by state law.

APPENDIX III

Resources

RECOMMENDED READING

Crouch, Holmes F. *Profits, Taxes & LLCs*. CA: Allyear Tax Guides, 2002.

Daily, Frederick W., and Bethany Laurence. *Tax Savvy for Small Business*. 8th ed. Berkeley, CA: NOLO, 2004.

Fershtman, Esq., Julie I. *Equine Law and Horse Sense*. Franklin, MI: Horses & The Law Publishing, 1996.

Jacobson, Patricia, and Marcia Hayes. *A Horse Around the House*. New York: Crown Publishers, Inc., 1978.

Klimesh, Richard, and Cherry Hill. *Horse Housing*. North Pomfret, VT: Trafalgar Square Publishing, 2002.

Lyons, John, with Browning, Sinclair. *Lyons on Horses*. New York: Doubleday, 1991.

Mancuso, Anthony. *The Corporate Minutes Book: A Legal Guide to Taking Care of Corporate Business*. 2nd ed. Berkeley, CA: NOLO, 2002.

Mancuso, Anthony. *Form Your Own Limited Liability Company*. 3rd ed. Berkeley, CA: NOLO, 2003.

Mancuso, Anthony. *Incorporate Your Business: A 50-State Legal Guide to Forming a Corporation*. 2nd ed. Berkeley, CA: NOLO, 2004.

Mancuso, Anthony. *LLC or Corporation? How to Choose the Right Form for Your Business*. Berkeley, CA: NOLO, 2005.

Mancuso, Anthony. *Your Limited Liability Company: An Operating Manual*. 3rd ed. Berkeley, CA: NOLO, 2003.

Swift, Sally. *Centered Riding*. North Pomfret, VT: Trafalgar Square Publishing, 1985.

Twelveponies, Mary. *There Are No Problem Horses, Only Problem Riders*. New York: Houghton Mifflin Company, 1982.

Tyson, MBA, Eric, and Ray Brown. *House Selling for Dummies*. 2nd ed. New York: Wiley Publishing, Inc., 2002.

Tyson, MBA, Eric, and Jim Schell. *Small Business for Dummies*. 2nd ed. New York: Wiley Publishing, Inc., 2003.

EQUINE SUPPLY CATALOGS

American Livestock Supply
613 Atlas Ave.
Madison, WI 53714
800-356-0700
www.americanlivestock.com

Dover Saddlery
PO Box 1100
Littleton, MA 01460
800-406-8204
www.doversaddlery.com

Medi-vet.com
Medi-Vet Animal Health, L.L.C.
71345 Ellis Road
Covington, LA 70433
800-668-9698
www.medi-vet.com

State Line Tack
19601 North 27th Ave.
Phoenix, AZ 85027
888-839-9640
www.statelinetack.com

EQUINE FENCING

Safe-Fence
J.L. Williams Company
PO Box 209
Meridian, ID 83680
800-843-3702
www.safefence.com

EQUINE INSURANCE

Asset Equine Insurance, Inc.
PO Box 185
Pilot Point, TX 76258
888-686-5662
www.assetequine.com

Markel Insurance Company
4600 Cox Rd.
Glen Allen, VA 23060
800-842-5017
www.horseinsurance.com

EQUINE TRANSPORTATION

Federal Motor Carrier Safety
Administration (FMCSA)
US DOT number registration/updates and
company safety profiles: 800-832-5660
Operating authority or ICC/MC
numbers: 202-358-7000
Insurance: 202-385-2423/2424
www.safersys.org

PERSONAL FINANCE

Credit Bureaus

Equifax
PO Box 740241
Atlanta, GA 30374
Report fraud: 800-525-6285
Order a credit report: 800-685-1111
www.equifax.com

Experian
PO Box 2002
Allen, TX 75013
Report fraud or order a credit
report: 888-EXPERIAN (397-3742)
www.experian.com

TransUnion
PO Box 2000
Chester, PA 19022
Report fraud: 800-680-7289
Order a credit report: 800-916-8800
www.transunion.com

Insurance Ratings

Note: You can also call your state's depart-
ment of insurance for rating information.

A.M. Best Company
908-439-2200
www.ambest.com

Fitch Ratings
800-893-4824
www.fitchratings.com

Moody's Investor Services
212-553-1653
www.moodys.com

Standard and Poor's Insurance
Rating Services
212-438-7280
www.standardandpoors.com

Weiss Ratings, Inc.
800-289-9222
www.weissratings.com

National Association of Insurance
Commissioners (NAIC)
816-842-3600
www.naic.org

National Committee for Quality
Assurance (NCQA)
888-275-7585
www.ncqa.org

Retirement and Investing

American Arbitration Association
335 Madison Ave.
Floor 10
New York, NY 10017-4605
800-778-7879
www.adr.org

National Association of Securities
Dealers, Inc.
1735 K Street, NW
Washington, DC 20006-1500
(301) 590-6500
www.nasd.com

North American Securities Administrators
Association, Inc.
750 First St., NE
Suite 1140
Washington, DC 20002
202-737-0900
www.nasas.org

Social Security Administration
Office of Public Inquiries
Windsor Park Building
6401 Security Blvd.
Baltimore, MD 21235
800-772-1213
www.ssa.gov or www.socialsecurity.gov

T. Rowe Price®*
100 East Pratt St.
Baltimore, MD 21202
800-638-5660
www.troweprice.com
(*Mutual funds / investment advice)

U.S. Department of Treasury
Internal Revenue Service*
Tax Assistance Line for Individuals:
800-829-1040
Tax Assistance Line for Businesses:
800-829-4933
www.irs.gov
(*IRS Publication 590, *Individual Retire-*
ment Arrangements, contains the complete
guidelines for IRAs and is available on the
Web site. You should obtain a copy of the
current publication each year as the guidelines may change from year to year.)

U.S. Securities and Exchange Commission
Office of Investor Education and Assistance
100 F St., NE
Washington, DC 20549
202-551-6551
www.sec.gov

REAL ESTATE AND GENERAL PROPERTY INFORMATION

Colonial Farm Credit
7104 Mechanicsville Turnpike
Mechanicsville, VA 23111
800-777-8908
www.colonialfarmcredit.com*
(*Features links to general agriculture, government agriculture, and agricultural commerce sites, as well as the "Farm Credit Locator," which will help you locate a Farm Credit Office that serves your area.)

National Association of Realtors®
30700 Russell Ranch Rd.
Westlake Village, CA 91362
805-557-2300
www.realtor.com

National Fire Protection Association
1 Batterymarch Park
Quincy, MA 02169-7471
617-770-3000
www.nfpa.org

National Pest Management
Association (NPMA)
9300 Lee Highway
Suite 301
Fairfax, VA 22031
703-352-6762
www.pestworld.org

National Rural Water Association
2915 South 13th St.
Duncan, OK 73533
580-252-0629
www.nrwa.org

U.S. Department of Agriculture
Cooperative State Research, Education,
and Extension Service
1400 Independence Ave., SW
STOP 2201
Washington, DC 20250-2201
202-720-7441
www.crees.usda.gov*
(*Features links to your local extension offices and a listing of all states and land-grant universities.)

U.S. Department of Agriculture
Farm Service Agency
Public Affairs Staff
1400 Independence Ave., SW
STOP 0506
Washington, DC 20250-0506
202-720-7809
www.fsa.usda.gov

U.S. Department of Agriculture
Forest Service
1400 Independence Ave., SW
Washington, DC 20250-0003
202-205-8333
www.fs.fed.us

U.S. Department of Agriculture
Natural Resources Conservation Service
Attn: Conservation Communications Staff
PO Box 2890
Washington, DC 20013
202-720-3210
www.nrcs.usda.gov

U.S. Environmental Protection Agency
Ariel Rios Building
1200 Pennsylvania Ave., NW
Washington, DC 20460
202-272-0167
www.epa.gov

U.S. Geological Survey
Water Resources Division and Earth
Science Information Centers (ESICs)
888-ASK-USGS
www.usgs.gov

BUSINESS

Council of Better Business Bureaus, Inc.
4200 Wilson Blvd.
Suite 800
Arlington, VA 22203-1838
703-276-0100
www.bbb.org

Federal Trade Commission
Office of Consumer and
Business Education
600 Pennsylvania Ave., NW
Washington, DC 20580
202-326-222
www.ftc.gov

U.S. Department of Labor
Frances Perkins Building
200 Constitution Ave., NW
Washington, DC 20210
866-4-USA-DOL (487-2365)
www.dol.gov

U.S. Citizenship and Immigration Services
20 Massachusetts Ave., NW
Washington, DC 20529
800-375-5283
www.uscis.gov

U.S. Patent and Trademark Office
Mail STOP USPTO Contact Center
PO Box 1450
Alexandria, VA 22313-1450
800-786-9199
www.uspto.gov

U.S. Small Business Administration
409 Third St., SW
Washington, DC 20416
800-U-ASK-SBA (827-5722)
www.sba.gov*
(*This website has information on writing
business plans, obtaining capital, employment issues, and links to agencies in your
state that may prove helpful.)

INDEX

Page numbers in *italic* indicate figures.